GW00854586

Deadly Fа

Written By David Pietras

Copyright © 2014 by David J. Pietras

http://mrdavepp.wix.com/davidpietras

Cover design by David Pietras

ISBN-13: 978-1495349027
ISBN-10: 1495349020

1 2 3 4 5 6 7 8 9 10 14

PROLOGUE

Cultist groups have permeated society ever since people could chat and share ideas en masse, although modern cult experts today often clash about what, exactly, makes a group of people a cult. What's a loony or eccentric organization to one expert is often seen by others as a religion or sect, which are terms loaded with less cultural stigma. Whatever the best working definition might be, here we present four of popular culture's craziest cults of our time.

One thing that baffles society is the fact that so many people choose to follow a single man and look to him as a messiah. Cult members usually refer to their leader as the reincarnation of Jesus Christ and obey his every command.

Some cults focus on doing good for society and the world in general yet others choose a more sinister path of murder and mayhem. And the ultimate cult following consists of mass suicides. Whatever the reasoning of these followers or the mindset of their leaders, one thing is definite. When deadly faith is your guide and destruction is your gospel, your own soul is your ultimate sacrifice.

David Koresh

David Koresh, 1987

A number of people, both witnesses and historians, have tried to accurately document the facts of what happened on February 28th, 1993 in Waco, Texas in the clash between law enforcement and a religious group known as the Branch Davidians. No one seems able to write about those events in an unbiased manner, since it seems that the whole thing was preventable. Even the academics appear to have a cause, so it's difficult at times to piece together what actually happened and who was to blame. Was Koresh a manipulative psychopath who exploited an opportunity, as many FBI agents claim, or was he just a deluded religious leader whose private play was suddenly exposed on the world's stage? Perhaps we'll never know.

Hostage negotiator Christopher Whitcomb, writing in *Cold Zero*, and true crime writer Clifford Linedecker in *Massacre at Waco, Texas* both present a chronology of the facts on that momentous Sunday morning.

Somewhere between 70 and 76 armed agents from the Bureau of Alcohol, Tobacco, and Firearms (ATF) prepared to move on a group of wooden buildings outside the central Texas town of Waco. Known as the Mount Carmel Center, the place was occupied by members of an apocalyptic religious group that was led by a man named David Koresh. Rumored to be stockpiled inside was an arsenal of explosives and weapons, some of which reportedly had been illegally converted to rapid-fire automatic.

That put them under the ATF's jurisdiction. A UPS driver had tipped off the government when a package bound for Mount Carmel had broken open to reveal casings for hand grenades. While the group did earn money from gun sales and were legally allowed to trade in arms, it appeared that they weren't following protocol. Some neighbors also reported a lot of target practice.

The Branch Davidians compound,
before the fire

But there was more, too, which came out in the days ahead. Linedecker claims that the local newspaper was running a series of articles about Koresh's dubious activities, entitled "The Sinful Messiah," based on accounts by defectors like Marc Breault, who later authored *Inside the Cult*. Breault had hired detectives to snoop around and when contacted by the ATF, he supplied a number of detailed descriptions of his former associates. He denounced Koresh, speaking of child abuse and polygamy.

Thanks to some of these leads, the ATF set up several agents to act as college students interested in Koresh's teachings. They moved into a house nearby and came over to visit. Catherine Wessinger, a religious scholar at Loyola University who penned *How the Millennium Comes Violently*, claims that they never fooled the Davidians.

Then that February 28th morning, a reporter asked for directions from a person who was connected to the Davidians, and that person alerted Koresh. At the time, one of the ATF agents was at Mount Carmel, and he left in a hurry. That behavior alerted Koresh, who was already aware that people had been asking questions about him. The agent who left called the ATF commander to let him know that the Davidians were aware of their approach. There was no more secrecy.

In fact, there never really had been. Since reporters either accompanied the agents or arrived before them at the target area, clearly they'd been alerted. Linedecker, writing from the ATF's point of view, said that it seemed early enough in the day to the commanders that surprise was still on their side. Besides, it was Sunday and the guns were supposedly locked up for the day of prayer. So the agents got into a convoy and drove out to the barren grounds to serve their warrants and seize any illegal items. A Blackhawk helicopter from the Texas National Guard accompanied them, along with two others belonging to the ATF.

Everyone was aware of the potential risk. Koresh's paranoia about the government as the agent of Satan didn't help matters, because the ATF's advance only proved the truth of his prophecies: they would be attacked by the Babylonians. Even so, no one anticipated what actually happened.

The Attack

The agents hoped that this incident could be settled
quickly. At nearly 10 o'clock, as three teams formed to
enter the building, an agent went to the compound's front
door and knocked. "The first entry team was to be inside
the front door within seven seconds after the convoy pulled
up to the compound," says Linedecker. "All the assault
teams would be deployed within thirteen seconds." They'd
been preparing for this for eight months, and each team had
an assignment—protect the children, neutralize the military
force, and seize the arms.

Koresh looked out from behind a steel door and learned
that the agents had a search warrant. Instead of letting them
in, he slammed the door and then someone started
shooting. It's not clear from which side the first bullets
came, but both sides commenced a fierce gun
battle. Wessinger says that survivors of the skirmish and

the subsequent standoff claimed that bullets came in through the ceiling, which meant that agents in the helicopters were firing into the compound. The ATF, in several hearings afterward, say no one in the choppers fired a single shot. By some reports, agents were shooting the dogs to get them out of the way and that's what started the deadly crossfire between the two groups. Women from inside who survived claimed they'd placed their bodies over the children to protect them from the rain of bullets.

Several agents were hit right away, and multiple shots came at the hovering choppers. One member of a team that penetrated the building was shot in the head and killed. Several who had climbed to the roof rolled off when hit. From noises inside, said agents in later hearings, it was clear that the cult had some heavy artillery. Bullets even pierced the reporters' cars and then concussion grenades, known as "flash-bangs" exploded among the agents. Koresh and his crew appeared to have superior weapons. They also had the advantage of cover, while the agents were out in the open.

Nevertheless, women were screaming inside and men were yelling. ATF bullets pierced the front door, behind which Koresh had been standing. Several people had been hit, including cultists firing from the tower, and four were wounded while five were dead. Whoever had started it, both sides knew they would have to fight hard for survival.

Confusion Reigns

The intense skirmish continued for around two hours before a truce was called, allowing the ATF to remove their dead and wounded. It turned out that 20 agents had been hit, but emergency facilities were 20 minutes away. The wounded were transported, but too late for four men, who'd sustained mortal wounds. (Wessinger claims the count was 20 wounded and four dead, but FBI records indicate that 16 were wounded and four were dead.)

ATF agents killed in gun battle

While the ATF waited through a tense afternoon, they arranged to make some statements over a local radio station, in the hope Koresh was listening, to let him know there would be no new attacks. Yet around 5:00 when three cultists walking outside the compound to return there from work encountered ATF agents, the shooting resumed. Agents killed one and captured one of the trio, while one got away, and officials then broadcast a request to Koresh to give up without a fight. His response was a scripture reading.

Wessinger interprets his behavior within her analysis of end-times religious groups by pointing out that his "ultimate concern" was to "obey God's will, as revealed in the Bible, in order to be included in the millennial kingdom." They had believed that day to be imminent and had armed themselves for its eventuality. Inside the buildings were over 100 people who believed in Koresh's divine gifts and his ability to dictate to them what God wished for them. Several apostates who were advising the ATF indicated that a siege could very well trigger a mass suicide like Jonestown. Nevertheless, ATF director Steven Higgens, as reported by Wessinger, had insisted two days before that a show of force against this group was necessary.

Koresh quickly contacted the media and participated in several live interviews with CNN about how the ATF had endangered his flock. He emphasized the number of children who lived in the compound and said that he'd been shot and was bleeding badly. He expected to die. (In fact, as Wessinger indicates, he probably interpreted this as another fulfillment of the prophecy of the lamb being mortally wounded.)

By that time, the ATF was reinforced, along with local police officers, Texas Rangers, members of the FBI's Hostage Rescue Team (HRT), the FBI's Special Agent in Charge (SAC) from the San Antonio office, a bomb squad, and several U.S. Marshals. The media, too, began to pour in. Koresh released four children ranging in age from three to six, and everyone settled in for a long night.

The Messiah

Former Davidian Marc Breault provides a long history of the development of the Branch Davidians as an offshoot from the Seventh Day Adventist Church. He also details how Koresh rose to power and eventually took over. In the beginning, his name was Vernon J. Howell and he was a high school dropout with the gift of the gab.

The Seventh Day Adventists advocated purity of the body as the temple in which the Holy Spirit resides, so their habits of eating and drinking were strict. They believed the final battle between good and evil could happen at any time, and when it did, and only a select number would witness the return of Jesus Christ and be saved. Yet some members wanted regulations to be even stricter, and from the original church several sects formed.

Within this congregation during the early 1930s, Victor T. Houteff preached about the approaching Apocalypse. He was chosen by God to cleanse the church, and when his defiant dogmatism forced him out, he took several followers with him. In 1935, they purchased land outside Waco, calling it the Mount Carmel Center. Then Houteff renamed his sect the Davidian Seventh Day Adventists, and when he died in 1955, his wife Florence succeeded him as leader. She gave a confident prediction for the exact date of the world's end in 1959, and many frightened converts flocked to Waco.

David Koresh in 1981

When her prediction proved false, Benjamin Boden then attracted a disillusioned group to himself. He called this group the Branch, which then became the Branch Davidians. When he died, his wife, Lois, became the new prophet, and among the more ambitious members of her group was Vernon J. Howell, who had joined in 1983.

He was easy-going, handsome, and aggressive, with the flamboyance of a rock star. He could take any Bible verse and discuss it endlessly, which made him seem highly intelligent, even gifted—possibly inspired. Lois Boden's son and heir, George, hated Howell. He intended to be the group's next leader, no matter how charming Howell might seem. There could only be one Messiah.

As these two faced off, Howell charmed the elderly Lois into taking him as a lover. He claimed it was God's divine command that they produce a child together, although they failed in this. Eventually the two men gathered their respective supporters, each claiming exclusive access to Biblical revelation. Howell insisted that as God's "seventh messenger," it was he who would set off the chain of events that would bring on the Apocalypse. In some ways, he was right, at least for his own flock.

When Lois died in 1986, Boden forced Howell out. Howell left for a while, but then returned for a face off. Boden had dug up the corpse of an elderly woman to challenge Howell to raise her from the dead, so Howell tried to use this incident to get Boden arrested. The sheriff needed proof, so Howell armed himself and took some men to enter Mount Carmel to get photographs. Boden came at them with an Uzi and they shot back. Surprisingly, no one was killed, but Boden quickly went to prison on an unrelated charge and that opened the door for Howell to take over. In a court trial, Boden appeared to be more dangerous—especially when he had the corpse brought into the courtroom to prove his powers. Howell was acquitted of all charges, and he saw this as a sign of God's protection. Boden left town and was later committed to a mental hospital.

Koresh with wife Rachel and
son Cyrus

Now Howell was free to affirm himself as a harbinger out of the Book of Revelations who could interpret the prophecies of the Seven Seals. When inspired one day by the "New Light," he divided husbands from wives and claimed all the women as his own. He gave each girl a Star of David, which Breault says was a symbol indicative of ownership. "That cheap piece of jewelry signified that a female belonged to the exalted House of David and was destined to become a Handmaiden to the Lord"—the "lord" in this case being Howell.

It was important, Howell said, that as God he had to spread his seed and create a divine army. Then he dubbed his male followers Mighty Men—the guards of King Solomon's bed—and they were to be his primary soldiers. It was estimated that he'd claimed at least 15 girls and women for his harem, some as young as 12.

In 1990, Howell changed his name to David Koresh to bring together the concept that he was an heir to King David and that his name meant death. He dictated strict rules about how his flock should spend their days, apparently changing those rules at whim, and he preached at his flock day and night. Yet he himself was above the rules. He could eat food forbidden to them, sleep till noon, and drink alcohol.

By 1992, Koresh was teaching his followers about martyrdom for the cause. At the same time, he was stockpiling food and collecting arms to defend himself against any attacks, whether from defectors or government agents—the "Babylonians." While Wessinger claims that there's no evidence that the Branch Davidians were actually using the guns they were selling, they clearly had a siege mentality. The cult managed to acquire sufficient supplies—especially in terms of instant storable meals--to last a year, if the need arose.

According to defectors, Koresh demanded to know from members of his group how far they were willing to go in defense of the true faith. The only way to serve God was to be willing to die. He even taught the children that suicide might one day be required and showed them how to do it with cyanide or a gun. Eventually he changed the name of Mount Carmel to Ranch Apocalypse.

The FBI Arrives

The first few days following the failed ATF raid, the government assembled a crisis management team to talk with the cornered Branch Davidians. In their "Report to the Deputy Attorney General on the Events at Waco, Texas," compiled in October that year, the FBI described their crisis management program for handling situations like this. Acting quickly, they determined what resources would be needed and selected people for a team. That meant negotiators, tactical personnel, support people, local law enforcement, consultants, and liaisons with the media. Special Agent-in-Charge Jeffrey Jamar took over, raising the hackles of the ATF, who later said they had never asked for help. By 5 o'clock p.m. on the second day, the FBI had a full command center operating, which they had set up in a hangar at a former air force base about a mile from the Branch Davidian compound. From the first day to the last, the place was abuzz with activity.

The Critical Incident Negotiation Team supervised the negotiations, using a team leader, an agent on the phone talking with someone inside the compound, secondary negotiators who handled that person's suggestions, and people to prepare the reports for the end of each day. These were kept in envelopes for anyone to read who might need information quickly.

The initial communications had occurred between ATF Special Agent James Cavanaugh and David Koresh, but then Lt. Larry Lynch of the Waco Police Department took over, speaking mostly with Steve Schneider and Wayne Martin, Koresh's trusted lieutenants. Schneider was a disaffected Seventh Day Adventist evangelist and Martin was an attorney. After the cult's messages to the media, the phone lines were rerouted from the compound so that anyone inside who dialed out would only get an FBI negotiator on the other end. During the second day, three negotiators kept up unceasing contact with 15 different members of Koresh's group, but that soon changed to contact with mostly Schneider or Koresh.

Outside, the job of the Hostage Rescue Team was to control the perimeter around the compound, for which they used different types of intimidating tanks. Christopher Whitcomb describes what it was like to be there, and he makes it clear that while the negotiators were trying to settle things peacefully, the HRT were ready for action. It was clear that the FBI's own people were working at odds with each other, and many of them knew it throughout the siege. Yet each side believed it was right: Negotiators insisted that tactical behavior only fulfilled Koresh's prophecy and strengthened his resolve, while the HRT people, with their pro-military mindset, believed that encroaching on his territory intimidated him and weakened him in the eyes of his flock.

Koresh informed the FBI that he'd been hit by two bullets, one through the hip and the other through his left wrist. He refused medical assistance. However, he did release ten more children that day, including a baby. The FBI believed there was hope that he might eventually give up, although a psychological consultant was convinced that Koresh himself would never surrender. God was not going to prison.

Then things got ugly. When Koresh realized he couldn't dial out to anyone except the FBI, he threatened more violence and hung out banners for requests for the media. Even so, he repeatedly assured anyone who asked that he had no plans for suicide. He promised to let everyone out if his message was played for the whole nation. As a show of good faith, he sent out a few more children.

Also as a show of good faith, the FBI made arrangements for the broadcast on March 2, while U. S. Marshals prepared to take people into custody. Then they awaited the hour-long tape that Koresh was making. It arrived at 8:00 a.m., along with the release of two more children and two adults.

As several Christian radio stations broadcast Koresh's speech, negotiators worked out the surrender logistics. Koresh was to come out first, carried on the stretcher. Then Schneider was to send someone out every two minutes. Vehicles were put in place to pick them up.

That afternoon, Koresh assured negotiators that the plan was proceeding. He just wanted to lead his people in prayer.

Then at 6:00, he said that God had instructed him to wait. There would be no surrender that day. Thereafter, all he offered were Bible readings and statements of resistance.

According to the FBI report, they learned that things were not as they had seemed. Even as Koresh had denied ideas about suicide, he had actually formed a rather insidious plan. According to one of his own followers, Koresh believed he was about to die so he'd instructed his group in what they were to do once he expired. They were to carry him outside on a stretcher and then fire on the agents so they would kill and then be killed. Some of them were given hand grenades, and allegedly Koresh had instructed them to stand together in small groups and pull the pins. That way they could take as many of "the Beast" with them as possible. Everyone was to die.

But then Koresh had a change of heart—perhaps because he was not dying, after all. After talking about meeting in the next world, the Davidians gathered to pray and to wait for further instructions. Koresh then advised them that they should not emerge at that time, because he had sinned by indulging in whiskey and prohibited food. That would effectively eliminate their salvation.

The standoff continued.

The Siege

The next day, Koresh reiterated that his commands came from God and he sent out one child with nine puppies. Then he offered more scripture interpretations. He told the FBI that if his "boss" took it into his mind to punish them for what they had done, it would be the start of World War III.

While the negotiators quickly grew bored with his endless hours of rambling speeches, they wanted to get as many children out as possible, so they listened patiently. Yet then Koresh indicated that his own children would not be coming out.

The FBI began to realize that this man was unpredictable. The negotiators consulted with several mental health experts and religious scholars, and there appeared to be little consensus, except that Koresh was likely to be dangerous if pushed too far. Since 1993, many scholars have tried to interpret the situation in retrospect, condemning the FBI for their lack of understanding. If only they'd been educated in Biblical passages, Wessinger says, they would have known what Koresh was communicating.

Jayne Docherty, a professor of conflict resolution, writes that a study of these religious groups indicates that "a propensity toward millennial beliefs appears to be imprinted on the human psyche." The roots of a violent encounter, such as that between the ATF and Branch Davidians, are inherently interactive. The group itself would probably not become violent without the catalyst of aggression or persecution. Such groups are easy targets for "normal" people to demonize, and as such, the set-up tends to invite a clash.

One psychiatrist, Park Dietz, who came to the command center early, read through all the reports and said that Koresh appeared to have antisocial and narcissistic traits, as well as paranoid and grandiose delusions. While some appeal to the rational side of his personality might work short-term, in the long run, his psychopathology would erupt. He could become dangerous. The best approach was to validate his ideas and get him to believe that his mission has not yet been accomplished.

While he warned the FBI to be consistent, it became clear to negotiators that much of the ground they gained in discussions with Koresh was lost through bad judgment.

Pete Smerick, a criminal investigative analyst, wrote a report to headquarters back in Virginia that the on-site commanders were moving too rapidly toward tactical deployment. He advised backing off with the tanks. The HRT was just making the situation more volatile.

"For years, Koresh has been brainwashing his followers in this battle between the church and the enemy," one memo read, "On February 28, his prophecy came true. Koresh is still able to convince his followers that the end is near, as he predicted. Their enemies will surround them and kill them."

It wouldn't be effective to use traditional hostage strategy in this situation. They weren't dealing with criminals but with a religious fanatic whose followers would do whatever he said. Even worse than the show of force was the way the FBI seemed to be punishing every good act that Koresh did. When he sent people out, Jamar did things like turn off the electricity or broadcast raucous music. Koresh was clearly annoyed by all of this and it was no wonder that he believed that God instructed him to resist rather than surrender. They were playing against his divinity, trying to weaken him, so he was reaching for all the symbols of his power. It was a no-win situation.

Even so, over the 51 days that the siege endured, the revolving teams of negotiators kept trying to resolve things peacefully and save the largest number of people possible. The behavioral science people were well aware that the HRT and other military-minded personnel viewed them as "soft," but they knew their job.

Hundreds of suggestions were faxed and mailed to them every day from people all over the country, and some "experts" even showed up.

One man from a nearby university wrote a letter to Koresh that he expected the FBI to deliver. In it, he said that Koresh was misreading the scriptures, and he pointed out several divine directives that would indicate what God was really saying.

Other people wanted to be allowed into the compound to argue the Bible with Koresh. They were well meaning, but they failed to understand the kind of person Koresh was. They believed he could simply be reasoned into a different position and then give up. A few more aggressive people even threatened to force their way in to either help Koresh or show him the error of his ways. In fact, on separate occasions, two men managed to accomplish this. They were welcomed inside to be proselytized, and they both left before the final days.

A man claiming to be Jesus's brother arrived from Florida to talk with Koresh, and another claiming to be Jesus himself said that he had to go in and set Koresh straight on who Christ really was. One well-known minister claimed that Koresh was possessed by a demon and needed an exorcism, which he offered to perform.

Many of these "interventions" amused the negotiators, but at the same time, they were well aware that fewer people were coming out and that Koresh could remain inside with his band for quite a long time—perhaps as long as a year. He had supplies stashed away, and water. The worst thing for his people was the cold nights without electricity, but so far, they were enduring that. They asked for milk for the children, which the FBI could hardly refuse.

Trying to resolve things quickly, the negotiators tried to put together a strategy that relied on those things that Koresh most wanted. They knew he had won in court against Boden, and that he appeared to be enjoying all the sudden fame, so they worked on that angle: The ATF had attacked, they could prove it from the crime scene, and Koresh could take them to court and win. He would then draw even more followers and the Branch Davidians would be known all over the world. They were already on the cover of the major news magazines and the world was watching. Koresh could parlay this into something beneficial for himself and his followers.

Yet even as they said these things to him, they were aware that he knew he had some other concerns: dead ATF agents, charges of polygamy and child abuse. He was likely aware that things would not go as easily as promised.

Trying to get around Koresh, the FBI made tapes of the children who had come out, showing they were cared for and urging them to appeal to their parents to join them. They sent these tapes into the compound, and each time they called the press together for a television broadcast, they turned the electricity back on so the

Davidians could see what they were saying. The agents expressed concern for their safety and clarified inaccurate speculations.

One other ploy was to record Koresh on the phone, and when his words seemed to undermine his preaching, they would broadcast that over a loudspeaker for the rest of the cult to hear. It was hoped that at least some of them—in particular the key lieutenants—would see the inconsistency and question their leader.

Yet on March 9, just over a week since the siege had begun, Koresh sent out a videotape on which he and Schneider had recorded interviews with people inside the compound. Each one expressed a firm desire to remain there. They were not coming out unless God ordered them to.

Ultimately, Koresh was in control. He would decide when he'd negotiate and when he wouldn't. The FBI would have to sit there and wait.

Impatience Breeds Anger

On March 12, Davidian Kathy Schroeder came out. When questioned, she denied any plans for suicide, yet when she tried calling back into the compound, she received no answer. She did admit that some people inside wanted to come out but were afraid of Koresh. They wouldn't leave until he told them to. That message was alarming. That meant that Koresh might well have a plan that exploited his group members' inability to act for themselves.

At that point Special Agent in Charge Jamar decided to shut off the electricity for good. Up until then, he'd allowed it to come on for short periods of time, but he was tired of all the dilly-dallying. This tactic angered everyone inside the compound and further annoyed the negotiators. Koresh rightly called it an act of bad faith, and Schneider said that the three people who'd been about to come out were now going to remain. A couple of days later, the tactical people placed bright lights outside the compound at night to make it difficult for those inside to sleep and stepped up the loud music as an annoyance. Wessinger lists the kind of music used as Tibetan Buddhist chants, bagpipes, seagulls crying, helicopters, dentist drills, sirens, dying rabbits, a train, and songs by Alice Cooper and Nancy Sinatra. (A rock group actually offered to come in and play music that they knew would be psychologically demoralizing, but their offer was rejected.)

Then the HRT drained the compound's diesel storage tanks.

More adults came out, and Koresh said he would send out no one else. Then the loudspeaker system failed, much to Jamar's frustration and to the negotiators' relief, although they later got it working again.

The crisis management team advised Jamar that since Koresh offered no specific time frame for surrender, the wait could be indefinite. At that point, the introduction of teargas was mentioned.

To avoid this, the negotiators made Koresh an offer: In prison he could communicate with his followers and make a worldwide broadcast on CNN. In order to have these privileges, Koresh and his people had to leave by 10:00 the next day, March 23.

Koresh rejected the deal and tore up the letter, and one more man emerged at this point. Schneider became more belligerent in his phone conversations and many at the command center felt that something negative was building.

On March 25, the FBI sent in an ultimatum: send a minimum of 20 people out by the end of the afternoon or they would begin to prepare for action. When no one emerged, the FBI removed motorcycles and other vehicles from in front of the compound.

Two days later, according to FBI documents, Schneider denied Koresh's self-professed divinity and hinted that the FBI might burn the building to get them out. That seemed like a rather enigmatic comment, perhaps even a hint of what was being discussed inside. Then several days were taken up with meetings between Koresh, Schneider, and two lawyers, one of whom had been hired by Koresh's mother. Once that was settled, Koresh decided that he wanted to spend Passover in the compound. Since he was the leader of a religious group, there was no real point in arguing. The FBI gave in and waited through the Passover period.

As it neared an end, Koresh announced that he would observe it for seven more days. Passover was officially at an end, but who could argue? Once again, it was clear that he was in charge.

By this time, it was clear to everyone that it was going to be one thing after another with him. He wrote and sent out several letters over the next few days that indicated he would never surrender or leave voluntarily.

By April 10, it appeared to be time to resume discussions about tear gas, and this time, the argument was presented to the newly-sworn Attorney General Janet Reno. Having only recently taken up the reigns, this was a difficult situation to be in. She asked for information about the gas, in particular whether it was harmful to children. She was assured that it was not.

The FBI wanted to use a substance called chlorobenzylidene malononitrile, or CS gas. They claimed that it was not flammable, but others sources insist that it is highly flammable. Since the FBI did not expect flames to be present, they might have believed there was little real danger. However, inside the compound, to warm things up at night and to read, the group was using kerosene lamps. It seemed reasonable to expect that someone might have thought of that, yet clearly no one did.

Even as these discussions were underway, there were a few intermittent conversations with Koresh, who offered more of what they called "Bible babble," and negotiations appeared to be stalled. Koresh was now saying that he needed time to write a manuscript on the meaning of the Seven Seals, and he was at work on that now. He asked for supplies to accomplish this, and the FBI sent those in.

He completed it on April 16. Yet still he did not come out. Some of his followers who managed to get out said that he had only completed work on the first seal, while the FBI believed he'd finished the entire manuscript and still resisted them. By that time, they'd had it. They no longer believed any of Koresh's promises.

On April 17, Reno approved the use of CS gas to end the six-week standoff. Apparently she felt that the negotiators had come to an impasse and that the sanitary conditions in the compound were deteriorating. She was thinking of the 23 children still inside. In addition to that, the operation was getting expensive, with no foreseeable end. Tear gas was uncomfortable, but it would not harm anyone. The HRT was instructed to insert it gradually over a period of 48 hours and then be ready to capture people as they emerged. Arrest warrants were obtained for every person known to be inside, and search warrants for the compound were in hand. Teams prepared to wash gas off the children as they emerged and to get them to safety.

On April 18, tanks continued to remove vehicles from the front of the compound. Tension was high, and it was clear that Koresh was upset, especially when they moved his black Camaro. He called the command center and said, "If you don't stop what you're doing, this could be the worst day in law enforcement history."

A sniper with a good view of the compound reported that someone from inside had hung a sign on a window that read, "Flames await." It was an ominous message. The negotiators weren't sure what it meant but they suspected that Koresh had a plan. They were soon to find out.

The Apocalypse

Just after dawn on Monday morning, April 19, the FBI phoned the compound to warn those inside about what was to occur. Linedecker provides a full description of what was said. It was not an assault, the FBI insisted, but a means for getting the Davidians to come out. This was the most uncomfortable tactic they'd used thus far, and if it didn't work, they could only resort to real aggression. Yet they believed that no one would long endure the harsh fumes of the gas. It burned the mouth, eyes, skin, and lungs to the point that any reasonable person would accept a way to escape it.

Armored vehicle at the compound

Three minutes after the initial call, two Combat Engineering Vehicles approached the buildings, punched holes into the fragile walls, and began to spray teargas through nozzles into the compound, propelled by noncombustible carbon dioxide. Nearby were an Abrams tank and nine Bradley vehicles, while choppers flew overhead, taking aerial photos. Everyone was under orders that if children were in any way endangered, the mission was to be aborted.

Abruptly, the Davidians opened fire at the tanks. Yet the teargas injection continued and CS grenades were thrown in through the windows. The walls of the buildings were no match for the tanks, and large holes appeared wherever the tanks were used. Then the vehicles pulled back for an hour to reload and went at it again. The Davidians responded with more gunfire. They also tossed the telephone out the front door, a sign that all negotiations had ceased—although survivors claim that the tanks had broken the phone lines. (At this point, if those who said they were using kerosene lamps were correct, and if the tanks had indeed knocked them over, the fires would already have started and spread. However, it would be several hours before that occurred, putting the claim into some doubt.)

The Texas wind was fierce that morning, which was not good for the tactical teams. The FBI continued to broadcast pleas for the Davidians to come out, hoping that at least the women with children would do so. They assured those inside that no one would be harmed, but the Davidians had already seen some of their fellow members led away in the days before in handcuffs and orange prison suits. That was yet another tactical error meant to display force.

Then just a few minutes after noon, the buildings quickly went up in flames and the fire spread fast. Agents close to the buildings heard gunfire, and they assumed that the people inside had decided to end it with a mass suicide. An HRT agent later claimed that he'd seen someone light a fire in front of the building, and several loud explosions inside erupted into a giant plume of black smoke that filled the sky. Helicopters flew back and forth, recording what they could, but no one knew how dangerous it might be to get close.

Branch Davidian compound on fire

Again a message was broadcast over the loudspeaker that Koresh should send his people out. Only nine emerged. One woman who came out, her clothing in flames, tried to go back in, but was caught by an ATF agent and brought to safety.

Firefighters arrived but the FBI made them keep their distance due to gunfire and the possibility of more explosions. Around 12:45, they entered the building and found numerous incinerated bodies. Most were well beyond immediate identification.

The negotiators, who had worked long hours to ensure a peaceful resolution, were stunned. They had predicted something along these lines if aggression of any kind were used. Even so, they had not imagined the magnitude of what did happen.

And now it was time to investigate the crime scene. For that, another team was called into action, and those agents whose work was done went home. They were aware there would be endless inquiries about how such an event could have occurred.

The Aftermath

By the end of that shocking day, 80 people were found dead, 23 of them children under 17. Koresh had fathered 14 of them. While rumors spread that Koresh himself had escaped through underground tunnels, his body was later identified by dental records. He'd been shot in the head.

Shell of Branch Davidian compound

Many of the victims had died from gunshot wounds and one child had been stabbed to death. Over 100 firearms were eventually recovered from the scene, and 400,000 rounds of ammunition. Wessinger states that many of them were still in their plastic wrappers, apparently scheduled for shipment rather than for use, but that's an interpretation without evidence.

It wasn't long before accusations were flung from both sides that the other side had started the fire, and the FBI brought to court what they felt was clear evidence that the Davidians had done it. They produced surveillance audiotapes of people inside the compound joking the day before about "catching on fire." On the actual day, there were recorded commands to "spread the fuel" and "light the torch," yet survivors who had escaped the compound claimed there had never been a suicide plan. Still, they could not explain why Koresh refused to come out for six hours after the introduction of tear gas.

The subsequent investigation showed that the fire had three points of origin, which would not have happened accidentally. One canister that had incendiary potential and that matched what the FBI was using was actually found in water, so it could not have started a fire. Yet if it was true that CS gas was flammable, then the amount pumped into the compound could easily have caught fire. The question was what was the true source of the fire? Had the tanks knocked over oil lamps? If so, why hadn't the fire begun earlier? No one seemed to have satisfactory answers, but everyone pointed the finger, including people who were not even there.

Nevertheless, there was no doubt that the initiating ATF raid was ill planned and completely unnecessary. Koresh could have been arrested peacefully away from the compound while a search was activated. Even if the ATF firmly believed that only an element of surprise would have allowed the plan to succeed, once that surprise was lost, they should have stopped and prepared for something else. There was little evidence of awareness of what the Davidians were all about, and it was clear that a paramilitary maneuver simply to inspect some guns was overkill. In a videotape for the History Channel, entitled "Cults," journalist Mike Wallace sternly points out that there were many people to blame for what happened to the Branch Davidians inside the compound, not just them, and there might never be complete clarity on the issue.

The ATF made another suspicious decision as well. On May 12, less then a month after the incident, they bulldozed the site. In other words, if there were any clues remaining after the fire that might have provided information as to what took place, they were now beyond use.

Most Americans afterward blamed the Branch Davidians for what had taken place, but in later years, the sentiment shifted somewhat, and some homegrown radicals decided there should be some payback. Only two years later, on the anniversary of the fire, Timothy McVeigh left a truck full of explosives outside the Alfred P. Murrah Federal Building in Oklahoma City, killing or injuring hundreds of workers and their children. Those who view the government the way Koresh did are unlikely to accept any explanation but one: unwarranted government persecution.

David Koresh had decided that the Fifth Seal of Chapter 6 in the Book of Revelation predicted that Armageddon would occur there at Mount Carmel. It describes those who were slain for the Word of the Lord and mentions a waiting period, after which the entire community would be killed. According to Koresh's understanding, through this violence, he and his people were to achieve salvation.

While there were predictions from religious and political scholars that another Waco was in the making among other secretive groups, the FBI did learn from this incident. The next time they were faced with a similar standoff the Freeman in Garfield County, Montana in 1996, they approached it much differently.

From March 25 to June 13, the FBI confronted a small group of Christian Patriots who called themselves the Freemen. Their aim was to overthrow the government, which they viewed as satanic. As part of a protest, some of them stopped paying taxes and government loans, which resulted in the foreclosure of their property. Instead of leaving, they tried setting up their own local government and threatened to arrest even to hang local government officials.

This brought in the FBI, but with restrictions from Attorney General Reno that there would be no armed confrontation. The Freemen that gathered on a foreclosed wheat farm were armed, but the federal agents relied on more than 40 negotiators, including family members of the protesters, to try to bring about a peaceful resolution. No one wanted another Waco. Those on the farm were offered conditions that allowed them to remain loyal to their concerns and to run their own defense even as 14 of them were taken into custody. In other words, contrary to Waco, the FBI avoided acting in a way that confirmed the group's persecutory belief system, and the matter ended in the courtroom for issues of tax evasion rather than on an impromptu battlefield.

The Heaven's Gate Cult

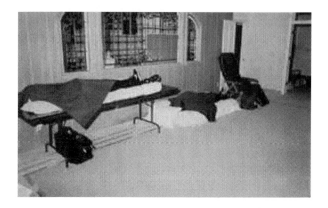

The mind of the fanatic, according to social philosopher Eric Hoffer in *The True Believer*, needs something to worship, even to the point of annihilation. He will sacrifice everything for the impossible dream. Many fanatical mass movements form in our society but only those that act in some dramatic manner, such as announcing the world's end or committing mass suicide, seem to get widespread attention.

Heaven's Gate was among the most startling.

A peaceful and secretive group, they made occasional forays into recruitment, but most of their time was spent in rigorous training for reaching a higher plane of consciousness. While there's nothing unusual about that, they are among the few cults who went all the way. To understand how they formed the beliefs that led to their ultimate actions, we need to look at cults as a whole that hold philosophies of an approaching Armageddon and a savior messiah.

"All mass movements," Hoffer wrote, "generate in their adherents a readiness to die and a proclivity for united action; all of them, irrespective of the doctrine they preach and the program they project, breed fanaticism, enthusiasm, fervent hope, hatred, and intolerance; all of them are capable of releasing a powerful flow of activity in certain departments of life; all of them demand blind faith and a single-hearted allegiance."

Cults that promise a higher order from such extreme discipline appeal to a certain type of mind:

Frustrated with the way things are

hungry for change

confident of the potential for human perfection

eager to believe in a single truth

able to envision an unprecedented society

ready for action

Religious scholar Catherine Wessinger calls the groups that form around these doctrines millennialists, and in *How the Millennium Comes Violently* she says that they're motivated by an ultimate concern: "the belief in an imminent transition to a collective condition consisting of total well-being, which may be earthly or heavenly."

Salvation is for the entire group, not just the individual, and it's generally ensured through a charismatic leader who knows how to socialize converts, reinforce beliefs and keep the group organized and focused. Monastic discipline, special diets, and social withdrawal cultivate dependence on the leaders and encourage the loss of individuality.

On A&E's program "Cults" Professor Charles Strozier at John Jay College of Criminal Justice added that "there's an important connection between what occurred in the 19th century and the latter part of the twentieth century in terms of movements of intense spirituality. There's been a large expansion of the number of people joining these groups and claiming they've received a message from beyond, in particular that we're not alone and can be helped to evolve toward greater insight and godliness."

Among them are:

> The Millerites, founded by William Miller during the nineteenth century, interpreted the Bible to say that the world would end with the Second Coming of Christ on October 22, 1844, but it did not. They awaited the arrival of a comet as a celestial sign of the world's end. Instead they ended up marking the day as "the Great Disappointment." They fixed on several more dates, but none played out as predicted, which discouraged many members. Eventually the lack of veracity in these predictions shriveled the group's numbers. However, some former members then went on to form the Seventh Day Adventists.

David Koresh, 1987

In the 1930s, Victor T. Houteff initially led the Davidians, an offshoot of the Seventh Day Adventists who awaited the imminent final battle between good and evil. When it occurred, only the chosen would witness the return of Jesus Christ and be saved. Houteff purchased land for his group outside Waco, Texas, calling it the Mount Carmel Center. When he died in 1955, his wife Florence succeeded him and erroneously predicted that the world would end four years later. When it did not, another group broke off, forming the Branch Davidians, which was eventually taken over by David Koresh. He called himself the messiah and selected girls among his flock who would bear his "soldiers." He insisted that as God's "seventh messenger," it was he who would set off the chain of events that would bring on the Apocalypse. When the group began to collect firearms, the ATF tried to raid the place in 1993, and after a 51-day standoff, Mount Carmel went up in flames, killing Koresh and approximately 80 of his followers.

Mount Carmel compound

In 1994, during a police investigation, 52 members of the Solar Temple were found dead in Quebec (Canada), and Switzerland. Fifteen appeared to have been true suicides, while others were lured into ingesting tranquilizers and then were shot. A few people who were regarded as traitors were summarily executed. In

1995, 16 more members of this cult were found dead in Grenoble, France, including three children. Fourteen of the bodies were arranged in a star pattern and burned. They left notes telling those who found them that they were going now to another world. They believed they were the reincarnated Knights Templar, a medieval holy order founded by nine French knights. Two years later in 1997, five additional members committed suicide. These believers thought that death was an illusion and upon leaving the Earth, they would receive solar bodies on Sirius, the brightest star in the universe.

Former Solar Temple in Switzerland

"Cults have been part of American life since the Pilgrims landed at Plymouth Rock," said TV journalist Mike Wallace in a documentary he made on the subject. Some are highly unorthodox, he added, and among the most bizarre was Heaven's Gate. Members of this group had an ideology crafted by a man and woman who believed they were aliens. For these two, people left families, jobs and friends to devote their lives to whatever it would take to attain ultimate spiritual perfection.

Whatever it would take.

Celestial Gurus

Marshall Herff Applewhite was the overachieving son of a
Presbyterian minister. He was always a classic leader who
could easily persuade people to accept his ideas and follow.
He had attended seminary, been a choir director, and had
numerous roles in the Houston Grand Opera, but was
dismissed from his teaching position at the University of
Alabama School of Music over an affair he had with a male
student. His wife left him, taking their two young sons, so
he got another job and once again got entangled with a
student, this time a young woman. In 1972, he admitted
himself into a psychiatric hospital, according to some
accounts, to cure his obsessions with sexuality. In his early
forties, he viewed himself as being seriously ill.

There he met a nurse, Bonnie Lu Trousdale Nettles, a
member of the Theosophical Society who was four years
older than him. At the time, her own marriage was falling
apart and she persuaded Applewhite that he could have a
major role in her work and her life. He listened and was
soon involved in her activities.

These two discovered a mutual fascination with UFOs,
astrology, and science fiction. Nettles urged Applewhite to
read *The Secret Doctrine* by Madame Blavatsky, and they
opened a center in Houston for the study of metaphysics.
They came to believe that they were the earthly
incarnations of aliens millions of years old: they were the
two witnesses mentioned in Chapter 11 of the book of
Revelation, placed on this earth to "harvest souls," i.e., to
help save as many people as they could. Nettles persuaded
Applewhite that as "The Two" they should embark on an
evangelical mission to bring the truth to others. Nine
months after they met, they severed ties with family and

friends (she left her four children) and drove out of Houston together to spread their message.

What they told people was similar to what many other end-times cult leaders preached: that they would be persecuted and put to death by their enemies, their bodies would lie in the open for three and a half days, and they would prove their deity by rising from the dead and disappearing into a cloud. From there they would ascend to a higher level to be with God. Their interpretation of the biblical "cloud" was that it was actually a spaceship, and they expected to be welcomed aboard. Indeed, this was their only means of salvation from the "Luciferians," who were evil aliens that enslaved humans through worldly concerns like jobs, sex, and families. Those who believed in the message could join The Two and be saved as well.

Before they could get much of a start, their invitation to the media for a press conference got them into real trouble. In Brownsville, Texas, Applewhite told a reporter that if he came to the press conference, they would give him the most significant story of his career. Believing it was about drugs, he brought the authorities. When The Two spotted the police, they left, which aroused suspicions. Officers looked up the license plate number of their rental car, discovered that it had been reported stolen, and arrested them.

They were charged with credit card fraud (charges were dropped) and car theft. Applewhite served six months in jail awaiting trial, and was convicted and sentenced to four more months. The judge ordered a psychiatric exam, which Applewhite passed but which he later admitted made him doubt his sanity.

Humiliated and even more paranoid when he left jail in 1975, he and Nettles went to southern California to start spreading the word. They called their group HIM, for Human Individual Metamorphosis, and picked up 25 disciples. Then they started their formal campaign in earnest.

The first official public meeting was scheduled in the seaside town of Waldport, Oregon in 1975. For months beforehand, they had posted fliers on telephone poles urging people to attend the meeting to discover the truth about reality. Two hundred people arrived at the Bayshore Inn to find out what the fliers were about.

The Two insisted that to be saved, spiritual-minded individuals must recognize that the appearance that most humans have souls is merely an illusion. Only those who truly had souls and were ready to be harvested by God would recognize the truth of the message. Once they did, they would give up their worldly clutter at once and follow a strict regimen. Using biblical notions about sexless angels and the praise Christ gave to those who sacrificed family life to follow him, they insisted that spiritual perfection came only at a price. One had to first see the truth about the evils around them and want desperately to free oneself.

Applewhite and Nettles didn't convince as many people as they had hoped, yet their strong belief in what they said, along with their intensity in delivering the message, proved compelling.

"They were a team act," said one former member about these gurus. "They played off each other."

"They were everyone's mom and dad," said another. "They made people feel protected and reassured."

The Two gave several televised interviews about their beliefs and the miracles they would perform, which brought them nationwide attention.

"We're going to stage, so that it can be witnessed," said Applewhite on a news broadcast, "that when a human has overcome his human-level activities, a chemical change takes place and he goes through a metamorphosis just exactly as a caterpillar does when he quits being a caterpillar and he goes off into a crysalis and becomes a butterfly."

That did not mean they would leave their bodies behind in graves, he insisted.

"We're going to be murdered and when we are, after three and a half days, we're going to walk up, just get right up, and you're going to watch us."

Twenty people from Oregon joined them. Some came home from the meetings believing they would soon acquire the kingdom of heaven and they made dramatic changes right away. One man and his wife actually left their 10-year-old daughter, certain she would get whatever she needed.

Once the believers were gathered together, they were told to get ready. Heaven awaited. The time was approaching. The world would soon see that it was foolish to ignore the message of The Two.

The End - Almost

In that same eventful year, Applewhite and Nettles gave a date for their departure into outer space. The eager disciples were in a campground at the time and they learned that a spaceship was arriving to pick them all up. They congregated on the specified night to await its approach.

It didn't come at the expected time, so they sat up through the night and continued to wait. Hours went by and nothing happened.

Marshall Applewhite

Finally, Applewhite apologized for his mistake and invited anyone who desired it to go ahead and leave. A few returned to their families, but others remained, opting to await the next opportunity. This was home now. There was nowhere else to go. They had sacrificed too much to just walk away and they wanted their higher destiny. Even when The Two reinterpreted their approaching resurrection to be metaphorical rather than actual (the media had "assassinated" them so they didn't really need to lie dead in the street for three days), many people still stayed and waited for the next set of instructions.

Applewhite and Nettles instructed those who remained to cut their hair, wear androgynous clothing—a uniform that would set them apart and also remove temptations of the flesh—and adhere to a strict regimen of training and preparation. The idea was that their physical bodies had to be trained toward eventual perfection as genderless, eternal beings. They needed these bodies to get into heaven.

The demands for members were daunting, which curtailed the cult's early success, but The Two believed that purging earthly ways was the only means for rediscovering the alien beings they truly were—all of them. There was to be no more sexual contact and no personal privacy. The members soon formed into an insulated community, sharing the same thoughts and repeatedly affirming the dogma and prophecies. They developed "crew-mindedness," as Applewhite called it, working together in one mind the way they might have to function on a spaceship.

During all this activity, two sociologists who heard about the group on the news infiltrated it and pretended to be potential recruits. After a few months, they left, having learned very little. They did not see the kind of indoctrination and coherence among members that would ensure endurance. Little did they know. The program was evolving.

Applewhite and Nettles taught their disciples that they were all related. Applewhite was their father and Nettles, who was an older alien that had inhabited an older human form, was their grandfather. The Two renamed themselves variously as "Guinea" and "Pig," "Bo" and "Peep," and finally "Do and "Ti." After they perceived that the media was distorting their message, they went underground. They had a plan to fulfill. Yet by the end of 1976, the group had diminished from around 200 adherents to only eighty.

A legacy of $300,000 bequeathed to them allowed them to keep going. To attract more people, they promised spaceship rides for $433 and they had dozens of takers.

Cult expert Steven Hassan says that the people involved in cults like these are typically intelligent and educated, but that a loving charismatic leader who presents beliefs for which there can be no reality testing manipulates them. A new identity takes over that is dependent on how the leader defines it. "The mind can learn," he adds, "and it can learn things that are abusive to the self."

Then in 1985, Ti died of cancer and was not physically resurrected as promised. Such a mundane death seemed out of keeping with the sacred doctrines of the two witnesses, and it was clear that she was not going to get into heaven with a perfected body. Applewhite had to repair the damage, so he continued to emphasize the discomfort that true believers have with mainstream American society and he said that Ti had gone on before them to get things ready.

It wasn't difficult to use social alienation to create what Messinger calls "a context in which it seemed reasonable for believers to exit Planet Earth." While devaluing life around them, Applewhite revised his philosophy to interpret their physical bodies as mere vehicles for the soul that had to be shed before they could board the spaceship. In fact, Applewhite now claimed that Ti herself would be piloting the "mothership" that would carry them to a better place. That made the idea even more familiar and inviting.

In 1993, Applewhite launched another campaign for advancing into something "more than human." Calling the group Total Overcomers Anonymous, he placed a large ad in *USA Today* to alert the American populace to the fact that the earth would soon be "spaded under" and they would have one last chance to escape. He went so far as to say that he was the alien that had been inside the body of Jesus Christ, but two thousand years earlier, the souls had not been ready. He had returned in the form of Applewhite to take those who were prepared, but he was still the very same alien with the very same mission.

He got a few more people aboard and then had to decide what to do next. In *The Secret World of Cults*, Sarah Moran says that after the travesty at Waco, Texas, in the spring of 1994, Applewhite spoke about Koresh, began to collect guns, and hinted at a similar form of persecution. To achieve peace and avoid the Earth's destruction, says religion scholar William Henry in *The Keepers of Heaven's Gate*, it was mandatory that they leave the planet...soon.

The Real End

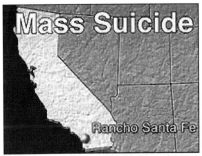

California map with Rancho Santa
Fe marked

In 1994, several members told a reporter for the *LA Weekly* that they would all be departing. They were going to walk out to the Santa Monica pier and catch a ride into space. But that did not take place, and in October of '96, they went to southern California, renting a large seven-bedroom house in the wealthy community of Rancho Santa Fe, north of San Diego, at 18241 Colina Norte. There they developed a computer business as Web page designers. They called the place "the Monastery" and their business "Higher Source." They also used the Internet's worldwide communication capabilities to promote their beliefs and gather more disciples. They renamed themselves Heaven's Gate. At this time, according to Wessinger, they had only around 25 adherents left in the group.

Rancho Santa Fe

On the Web page, Applewhite posted six key points, paraphrased as:

I and my partner are from the Evolutionary Level Above Human and we took over two human bodies in their forties, which had been tagged at birth as vehicles for our use.

We brought a crew of students to Earth with us from the Kingdom of Heaven.

Many of us arrived in staged crashes of spaceships and authorities confiscated some of our bodies.

Others came before us to tag our bodies with special chips.

Before our human incarnation, we were briefed by older beings with details about how to take over the human vehicle.

The Kingdom of God is genderless, multiplying through metamorphosis, and its inhabitants have free will.

Heaven's Gate logo

There were more messages regarding Earth's impending demise, and once again, a few people left everything to grab their "last chance" and join the cult.

Then in November and December of 1996, a comet called Hale-Bopp made a big splash, not just for Heaven's Gate but for the entire New Age community and beyond. Its last visit had been in 2200 BC, which was viewed then as a harbinger for the arrival of a great teacher, or Peacemaker, who would visit many different civilizations around the world to deliver a sacred doctrine. He would bring purification and save true believers from the tribulations of the end times.

It's no wonder that many who knew about this viewed the approach of the comet as a sign of great change.

One amateur astronomer said that a ringed object was following the comet, which was four times the size of Earth and which had thrown the comet off its course several times. It was even said that the Vatican was looking for some sign in the heavens, since this would be the last comet of the millennium. It supposedly signaled the final three years of Satan's reign on earth and would usher in a more enlightened age.

Do told the group that Ti had communicated telepathically to him that it was time and that Hale-Bopp was the sign. On their Web page they excitedly announced Hale-Bopp's approach.

Dr. Courtney Brown, claiming to be adept at "remote viewing," or seeing things that occurred far away, told radio host Art Bell that he was in possession of photographs of the comet. They clearly showed an object in its wake and this object had all the appearances of an alien craft. In fact, Brown said he'd "looked" inside and had seen alien life forms. This claim drew many expectant listeners who wanted to see the photos, including members of Heaven's Gate.

Hale-Bopp comet

Sensing the arrival of the most significant event in their short history, the crew-minded group went together to watch *Star Wars*. They also attended a UFO conference, bought insurance against alien abductions and impregnation, and purchased a high-powered telescope. They were looking for the "companion" to Hale-Bopp, they told the store manager, which they described as a small shape near the comet. That was their mothership. When they failed to find it, they returned the telescope. The manager found their ideas puzzling.

Then in January 1997, the promised photographs were finally posted on Art Bell's Web site and then were quickly exposed as a hoax. Yet the Heaven's Gate crew was not deterred. On their Web site they wrote, "Whether Hale-Bopp has a companion or not is irrelevant from our perspective." Its approach alone was significant as "the marker we've been waiting for." Visible or not, the spaceship would be there ready to take them home. They were about to "graduate" from human to more-than-human. Those who were reading the message might even want to get their own "boarding passes."

By the end of that month, on January 23, a remarkable celestial event occurred: the outer planets of our solar system aligned themselves in what many people said was a six-pointed star. That was the Jewish star, the symbol of Jesus. The last time this alignment had occurred had been just before the Renaissance. There was every reason to believe that something of universal significance was about to occur.

Death Mansion

On Friday night, March 21, 1997, the members of Heaven's Gate went to a chain restaurant called Marie Callender's, where they ordered 39 identical meals of salad and pot pies, and finished off with cheesecake. This was to be their final earthly meal, because the next day, the comet would be in its closest proximity to Earth. It was time to begin their departure.

On Saturday, they started the process. Everyone dressed identically in black long-sleeved shirts and black sweat pants, with new black-and-white Nike tennis shoes. On their left shirtsleeves were armband patches on which the words "Heaven's Gate Away Team" were stitched— possibly a reference to the television program *Star Trek: The Next Generation* on which a small crew called the "away team" went off on planetary ventures. The members of Heaven's Gate each packed a small overnight bag with clothing, lip balm, and spiral notebooks, and they placed these bags at the foot end of their beds. They also put three quarters and a five-dollar bill into their shirt pockets—a habit they had developed whenever they went out so they would always have cab fare or change for the phone. The Nike slogan at the time was "just do it," which could explain why they all wore Nike shoes.

They worked in three teams. The first team of 15 received the barbiturate phenobarbital mixed into pudding or applesauce. They then drank vodka to wash it down. A lethal dose was some 50 to 100 pills. It's surmised that after consuming this toxic mix, they lay on their beds with plastic bags over their heads until they passed out. Those who still lived removed the bags and covered their bodies with purple shrouds. The following day, Sunday, the next team of fifteen followed. Finally there were seven on Monday, and then only two.

The final two people, both women, were not shrouded but they had placed plastic bags over their heads to assist them in dying.

Two videotapes were sent by federal express to former members, who realized what had occurred and alerted police.

Victims in Jonestown, Guyana

Deputy Sheriff Robert Bunk went over to the mansion on the afternoon of Wednesday, March 26. An overpowering stench indicated the presence of corpses, so he called for back-up. Together, the two officers entered the home. Now they knew for sure there were bodies and remembering Jonestown, they wondered about some kind of mass murder. Yet they soon realized that the deaths there had been peaceful, voluntary, and surprisingly uniform.

"I've never seen anything like this in my life."

Mansion of death
yields 39 bodies

■ Members of religious group discovered dead in Rancho Santa Fe
■ Deaths appear to be a mass suicide, according to sheriff's deputies

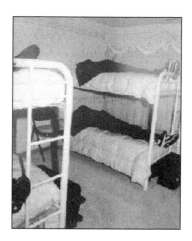

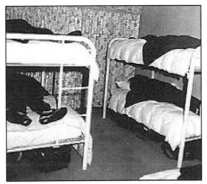
Cult member corpses in the house

There were 39 bodies lying on ordinary cots or bunks. Because they were all dressed alike with their hair cropped short, the investigators assumed they were all male and reported that to headquarters. The news media spread this as well. However, it turned out that among the victims were 21 women and 18 men, all white, from ages 26 to 72. Most had joined during the seventies, but eight had joined more recently during the nineties. It was the largest mass suicide to date to occur within the United States.

The place was eerily quiet as the San Diego County coroner went from one room to another, videotaping the scene. Twenty white plastic trash bags were found piled in the trash, along with elastic straps. On computer screens throughout the mansion were images of alien-human hybrids, along with one screen flashing a "Red Alert" from the Heaven's Gate Web site. Hundreds of videotapes found there featured cult members speaking to people they had left behind about how excited they were to be joining Ti on a higher plane. Clearly, each person had died of his or her own free will and had wanted very badly to do so.

Then San Diego County medical examiner Brian Blackborne announced another shocking find: seven members of the cult had been castrated, including Applewhite. Former cult members admitted to reporters that, yes, Do had done that and others had followed his example. It was all part of crew-mindedness and the battle against the Luciferian influence.

Professor Strozier at John Jay College said that Applewhite clearly had issues with sexuality, and other members who strongly identified with him would feel that they had to do whatever he did. It was all part of losing their individual identities.

The bodies were finally released to grieving and perplexed next-of-kin. Some openly said that their relative had done what seemed best, while others thought the cult member had been brainwashed and would never otherwise have committed such an act.

Then there was yet another shock. On Easter Sunday, March 30, writer Lee Shargel told David Brinkley on a television talk show that Applewhite had cancer. People who heard this wondered if he had led 38 other people into taking their lives simply because he had nothing to lose and didn't want to go alone. Yet autopsy reports showed no sign of cancer in his body. Shargel was a fiction writer. Had he just made that up? No one knew.

Wayne Cooke, 56, a former cult member known as Justin, appeared on *60 Minutes* with Lesley Stahl to talk about his experience with Heaven's Gate and his feelings about missing the "graduation." There were tears in his eyes as he described what the departure meant and how much he wished he'd gone, too. In fact, his wife had been one of the thirty-nine.

Five weeks later on May 6, he and another former member, Chuck Humphrey, 55, both dressed in dark clothes, packed a bag, pocketed five dollars and three quarters, and used the same drugs to take their lives in a hotel room in Encinitas. Cooke succeeded, but Humphrey survived. In a videotape, Cooke told his surviving daughter he had to follow his wife. "I'm just really happy," he said.

Humphrey decided that he'd been held back to continue to proselytize, so he created a Web page to dispense Heaven's Gate theology. He did as much as he thought he could to get the word out, and then in February 1998, he ended his life in the Arizona desert. He placed a plastic bag over his head and used his car's exhaust to fill it with carbon monoxide. Dressed in black with the requisite "fare," he left a purple shroud on the seat next to him with a note that said, "Do not revive." He called his suicide "an opportunity for me to demonstrate my loyalty, commitment, love, trust and faith in Ti and Do and the Next Level."

It's unlikely that the full story will ever be known and the mystery of the 39 suicides will become a permanent part of weird Americana. Yet one thing about Heaven's Gate does stand out. Unlike many cults who are criticized for warping young minds, no one who "graduated" to the "next level" took children along for this ride. Only adults, they believed, could make such a decision. They did not leave to escape persecution or hardship, and in fact had a luxurious home and a thriving business. It seems they simply wanted to catch a ride while they still could and move on to another truth.

Jonestown Massacre

The first reports out of Guyana on November 18, 1978
were that Congressman Leo J. Ryan and four other
members of his party were shot and killed as they
attempted to board a plane at Port Kaituma airstrip. Within
hours, came the shocking announcement that 408 American
citizens had committed suicide at a communal village they
had built in the jungle in Northwest Guyana. The
community had come to be known as "Jonestown." The
dead were all members of a group known as "The People's
Temple" which was led by the Reverend Jim Jones. It
would soon be learned that 913 of the 1100 people believed
to have been at "Jonestown" at the time had died in a mass
suicide.

According to the official report submitted to the U.S.
House of Representatives on May 15, 1979, the chain of
events leading to Leo Ryan's death in Guyana began a year
earlier, after he read an article in the *San Francisco
Examiner* on 13 November 1977. The article entitled
"Scared Too Long" related the death of Sam Houston's son,
Bob, in October 1976. Houston had decided to speak out
about his son's death because he believed that the reason

Bob had died, beneath the wheels of a train, was because he had announced his decision to leave the People's Temple the day before. Houston was also concerned that his two granddaughters, sent to New York for a vacation, had ended up in "Jonestown," Guyana and never returned.

Over the ensuing six to eight months, Ryan would hear more about the People's Temple through newspaper articles and from direct requests for assistance from concerned families whose relatives had disappeared into the Guyana jungle to join the "Jonestown" community. There were claims of social security irregularities, human rights violations and that people were being held against their will at "Jonestown." In June 1978, Ryan read excerpts from the sworn affidavit of Debbie Blakey, a defector from "Jonestown," which included claims that the community at "Jonestown" had, on a number of occasions, rehearsed for a mass suicide. After meeting with a number of concerned relatives, Ryan's interest in the People's Temple became widely known and the reports about the group, both favourable and unfavourable, began to pour in. He hired an attorney to interview former People's Temple members and the relatives of members to determine whether there had been any violations of Federal and California state laws by the group.

In September 1978, Ryan met with Viron P. Vaky and other State Department officials to discuss the possibility of Ryan making a trip to "Jonestown" in Guyana. This request was made official on 4 October. Permission was granted and the trip was planned for the week of November 12-18. Ryan's intention to visit "Jonestown" soon became widely known and the numbers wishing to accompany him had grown substantially. By the time of his departure there were nine extra media people and 18 representatives from a delegation of Concerned Relatives who would go with him, at their own expense. The official party, or Codel, consisted of Ryan, James Schollaert and Jackie Speier, Ryan's personal assistant.

In the days of preparation for the trip to "Jonestown," Ryan contacted Jim Jones by telegraph to inform him of his intention to visit the settlement. Through the U.S. Embassy in Guyana, Ryan learned that agreement for the visit was conditional. Ryan would have to ensure that the Codel was not biased, there would be no media coverage of the visit and Mark Lane, the People's Temple legal counsel, would have to be present. On 6 November, Lane wrote to Ryan and informed him that he would not be able to attend at the time they wanted, and claimed that the Codel was nothing more than a "witchhunt" against the People's Temple. Ryan responded with a declaration of his intentions to visit the settlement anyway and that he would be leaving on 14 November.

Problems began for the group as soon as they arrived in Guyana at midnight. Ron Javers from the *San Francisco Chronicle* was detained overnight at the airport, as he did not have an entry visa. The group of Concerned Relatives, despite having confirmed reservations, had to spend the night in the lobby of the Pegasus Hotel in Georgetown, because there were no rooms available for them. Over the next two and a half days, Ryan met with Embassy personnel and organised a meeting with Ambassador Burke and the Concerned Relatives. He and the family members attempted to speak with a representative of the People's Temple at their headquarters in Georgetown, but could not gain entry. In addition, Ryan was unable to negotiate successfully with Lane or Garry, another legal representative of the People's Temple, resulting in the postponement of the scheduled flight to the mission until Friday 17 November.

The negotiations still had made no headway on Friday morning, so Ryan informed Lane and Garry that he and his party would be leaving for "Jonestown" at 2:30 pm. There were two seats on the plane if Lane and Garry wished to leave with them. The plane left as scheduled at 2:30 pm that day. On board were Ryan, Speier, Deputy Chief of Mission, Richard Dwyer, Lane and Garry, all nine media representatives, four representatives of the Concerned Relatives group, and Neville Annibourne, a representative of the Guyanese Government.

At the Port Kaituma airstrip, Corporal Rudder, the Guyanese Regional Officer of the Northwest district, met the plane. His instructions from "Jonestown" were that only Lane and Garry were to be allowed to leave the plane. Negotiations as to who would be allowed entry into "Jonestown" then ensued between Ryan and "Jonestown" representatives who were at the airport. Eventually it was agreed that all but one media representative could go. Gordon Lindsay, consulting for NBC on the story, was denied entry because of an article he had written in the past that had criticised the People's Temple.

Upon their arrival at "Jonestown," the delegation was served dinner and entertained by a musical presentation by People's Temple members. As the evening progressed, reporters interviewed Jim Jones while Ryan and Speier talked to People's Temple members whose names had been provided by relatives in the U.S. During the course of the evening, a "Jonestown" member passed a note to NBC reporter Don Harris indicating that he and his family wished to leave. Another member made a similar verbal request to Dwyer. Both requests were reported to Ryan.

At 11:00 pm, the media and family representatives were returned to Port Kaituma as Jim Jones refused to allow them to spend the night on the compound. Ryan, Speier, Dwyer, Annibourne, Lane and Garry were the only ones who spent the night of Friday, 17 November at "Jonestown."

Back at Port Kaituma, local Guyanese, including one police official who told stories of alleged beatings at "Jonestown", approached media representatives. They complained that Guyanese officials were denied entry to the compound and had no authority there. They also described a "torture hole" in the compound.

The media and relatives were not returned to "Jonestown" until 11:00 am the next day, several hours later than planned. Ryan had continued interviewing members since early in the morning, during which time more individuals told of their desire to leave. By 3:00 pm there were a total of 15 People's Temple members climbing into the trucks with the delegation to drive to Port Kaituma airport. Ryan had intended to stay but was attacked by a People's Temple member, Don Sly, with a knife. He was not hurt but Dwyer insisted that Ryan leave with them. Dwyer planned to return to "Jonestown" later to resolve a dispute with a family who was split on the question of leaving Jonestown.

The party arrived at Port Kaituma airport at about 4:30 pm but the two planes did not arrive until about 5:10 pm. The delay had been caused by the unexpected request to the US Embassy for a second plane to carry the extra fifteen passengers. Soon after its arrival, a six-passenger Cessna was loaded and ready to leave. As it began to taxi to the far end of the airstrip, one of the "Jonestown" defectors on board, Larry Layton, opened fire on the other passengers.

At the same time, as Ryan's party were boarding the other plane, a twin-engine Otter, occupants of a tractor and trailer owned by the People's Temple, opened fire. Ryan, three members of the media and one of the defectors were killed. Speier and five others were seriously wounded. The shooting lasted between 4-5 minutes and the larger plane was disabled. The Cessna was able to take off and reported news of the attack to controllers at the Georgetown tower. They in turn notified the Guyanese officials. The attackers left the airport soon after, while survivors of the attack sought cover and protection for the night.

Congressman Leo J. Ryan's plane after the attack

According to the official report, the mass suicide began at about 5:00 pm as the shooting was beginning at the airport. At about 6:00 pm, Ambassador Burke was informed of the shooting. He, in turn, informed the US State Department at 8:30 pm by cable. At approximately 7:40 pm, Guyanese police told Sherwin Harris, a member of the Concerned Relatives Group, that his ex-wife Sharon Amos and three of her children were found dead at the People's Temple headquarters in Georgetown.

Word of the deaths at "Jonestown" reached Port Kaituma at about 2:00 am on Sunday morning when survivors Stanley Clayton and Odell Rhodes arrived there.

Congressman Leo J. Ryan

At dawn, Sunday, 19 November, the first contingent of Guyanese Army rescue forces arrived in Port Kaituma. More soldiers arrived within the hour. Their arrival later in the morning at "Jonestown" confirmed earlier reports of the mass suicide. The first Guyanese rescue aircraft landed at Port Kaituma, without medical supplies or personnel, at about 10:00 am. All of the wounded and most of the survivors were airlifted from Port Kaituma before nightfall and transferred to US Air Force medical evacuation aircraft in Georgetown.

A Time to Die

As Ryan's delegation was preparing to board their aircraft, Jim Jones called the "Jonestown" community together. He explained to them, as if it were a premonition rather than foreknowledge, that someone on the plane was going to kill Ryan. The consequences of this action would be that those political forces that had been trying to destroy the People's Temple for years would attack the people at "Jonestown". The "enemy" would descend upon them and kill them mercilessly. This was not a new threat to the community at "Jonestown," they had lived in fear of an unnamed enemy and destroyer for many years, nor was Jones's solution new to them. He had been preparing them for what he termed "revolutionary suicide" for some time. They had even had a number of practice runs to prepare them for just such an event.

The scene of the massacre at
Jonestown

A tape-recording of the mass-suicide reveals that there was little dissent about the decision to die. One or two women who felt that the children should be able to live protested, but they were soon reassured by reminders of the alternative undignified death at the hand of the enemy and the shouted support of the group. The poison-laced drink was brought to the hall and dispensed. The babies and small children, over two hundred of them, were first, with the poison poured into their mouths with syringes. As parents watched their children die, they too swallowed the fatal potion. The moments before the final decision to die brought resistance from a few, but armed guards who surrounded the room shot many of them. Of the estimated 1100 people believed to have been present at "Jonestown" at the time, 913 died, including Jim Jones; the rest somehow escaped into the jungle. It is not certain whether Jones shot himself or was shot by an unknown person.

The most puzzling question, which has arisen out of the tragedy at "Jonestown", is how one man could achieve such control over a large group of people to the point that they would willingly die at his command. It would be easy to assume that "Jonestown" was a unique situation that could only have occurred because of Jim Jones's dynamic and charismatic personality, combined with the weakness and vulnerability of his victims. Such an analysis may bring some peace that such a thing could never happen again, but it falls a long way short of providing true understanding of the situation, thereby leaving us all vulnerable to the danger of further tragedies such as "Jonestown" occurring.

A view of Jonestown

To properly understand "Jonestown," it is necessary to explore the social and psychological processes that were employed which ensured that such extremes of social conformity and obedience were achieved. They are processes that are common in all social groups, but in instances such as the People's Temple, they were used to the extreme, with corresponding extreme results.

Members of the People's Temple had been trained for many years in readiness for the mass suicide that had finally occurred in November 1978. Jim Jones had shared with his followers his paranoid belief that the American government was plotting to destroy anyone who was involved in the People's Temple. Jones's followers were accustomed to looking to Jones for salvation. Over the years, Jones had introduced many outside "threats" to the safety of his followers but he had always removed the danger for them. Time and time again he had rescued them, they had learned to trust this man known to them as "Father."

Jones and his followers had moved to "Jonestown" with the vision to create a completely self-sufficient community based on the ideals of socialism and communalism. Each person would work for the common good, providing food, shelter, clothing, health care and education for themselves. In this community everyone would be equal and could live in peace. It was a noble ideal. One, as Jones would constantly remind them, which was worth dying for.

By November 1978, the people of "Jonestown" were ready to die. After many years of input, which had held such action as something to be aspired to, with no input negating such a belief, the members of the People's Temple would have easily seen their own deaths as an act of nobility and dignity.

The Visionary

Over the twenty years preceding the events at "Jonestown," the Reverend Jim Jones's number of followers throughout America had grown considerably, as he drew to himself the outcasts of society, along with those who desired to help the downtrodden and serve those in need. During the early 1960's, Jones preached the need for racial brotherhood and integration, an unpopular doctrine at that time which brought him much criticism from the church hierarchy. To avoid such criticism, Jones founded the People's Temple in 1963, where both black and white worshipped side by side. The poor and society's misfits were welcomed with open arms. Jones's congregation worked to feed the poor, find employment for the jobless and help ex-criminals and drug addicts to put their lives back together.

As Jones's congregation grew, so too did the demands he made upon his flock. Greater sacrifices and dedication were required of the People's Temple membership. As criticism of the church's practices increased, Jones relocated to northern California in 1965, along with 100 of his most dedicated and faithful followers. Once in California, the People's Temple grew considerably until there were several congregations, with its headquarters based in San Francisco.

To attract new members to his "church," Jones widely publicized his services, promising miraculous healings where cancers would be removed and the blind made to see. Upon arrival, potential recruits would witness a community of brotherhood and fellowship where everyone, no matter their social standing or color, was treated as equals. Each new potential member was greeted with personal warmth rarely encountered in the more traditional churches. People's Temple members would stand before the crowd and recount stories of illnesses that Jim Jones had cured for them. To further convince his audience of his great powers he would make predictions of events that would always come to pass, and receive "revelations" about members or visitors, things that only they could have known. Before their eyes, Jones would heal cancer patients and a mass of putrid tissue would be torn from the patient's body.

The passing of a severe initiation was required by new members that had the effect of making entry that much more desirable. Something that has to be earned is naturally valued more highly than that which is obtained freely. It also had the effect of creating a much higher level of commitment from members. Each new level of commitment asked of the member was immediately justified by the fact that much had already been sacrificed. To reject the new situation would mean admitting that the previous acts of commitment had been wrong. It is a natural phenomenon that people will tend to prolong a previously made commitment, even when painful, rather than admit that they had been mistaken.

The demands made upon a new member were only small and the level of choice was high. The commitment of further time and energy into the organization was gradual; the desire to do so was increased by the promise of the achievement of a higher ideal. All members were taught that the achievement of this ideal required self-sacrifice. The more that was sacrificed, the more that would be achieved. The new members would gradually come to see the long meetings and hours of work done for the church as being worthwhile and fulfilling. Jones increased his demands on the member only in small increments. At each new level of commitment, any reservations the person may have had could be easily rationalized and justified. By the time Jones's demands had become oppressive, the individual members were so heavily committed that to not fulfill any new demands would require a complete denial of the correctness of all past decisions and behavior.

Just as the demands on a member's time increased gradually over time, so did the level of financial commitment. In the early days of membership, giving money was completely voluntary, although the amounts given were recorded openly. By recording the amounts given, an unspoken expectation was conveyed. The new member could choose to give nothing or very little, but knew that his level of commitment was being measured. Over a period of time, the level of contribution was increased to 25% of each person's income and was no longer voluntary.

The highest level of commitment that could be demonstrated was when an individual or family lived at the People's Temple facilities, handing over all personal property, savings, and social security checks to the Temple. The ideal of communal living was a large aspect of Jones's teaching as being the only truly spiritual ideal. The outside world of capitalism and individualism was seen as evil and destructive. Forces of that evil system would see the ideals and achievements of the People's Temple as a threat to its own stability and thereby want to destroy it. Through such teachings, Jones was able to create the illusion that the only place of safety and comfort was the People's Temple. The member saw any criticism of the church from the outside as being untrustworthy and proof of what Jones had taught.

From the earliest stages of their indoctrination each member was taught that the achievement of a higher spirituality would require a struggle against their own weaknesses. Any areas of resistance an individual harbored against the church were quickly suppressed as being an indication of that person's lack of faith. Jones would regularly bring critics before the assembly and chastise them for their 'unbelief.' He would then require other members of the group to mete out the necessary punishment. Parents would publicly beat their children for transgressions while husbands and wives would be required to punish each other. In this way, each person was made personally responsible for the action and had to find a way to justify and rationalize it. In this way, Jones was able to become more and more brutal in his punishments as each member had learned to internalize the belief that such punishments were necessary and just.

The desire to relinquish more and more control of their lives over to Jones was further encouraged by the new-found harmony and peace that committed members found in their lives. Disputes within families gradually diminished. There was no longer any cause for disagreement since the rules were clearly laid down by Jones. The everyday stress, and sometimes even turmoil, they had known in the past from the constant need to make decisions and choices was now gone. Life was easier with fewer choices.

Any idea about leaving the People's Temple was quickly dismissed by the individual for a number of reasons. Their total commitment to the church usually meant that they had isolated themselves from their family and friends, whether from lack of association or open enmity. To leave the fold of the church would mean either admitting their mistakes to family and friends or being alone without any support group. Church reaction to, and retaliation against, other defectors who were hated as traitors and enemies would also make leaving difficult. To deliberately put themselves into a situation of being despised by their friends was extremely daunting; especially when for so long the People's Temple had come to be seen as the only safe haven from an evil world. The final barrier to emancipation was economic. Each individual had surrendered all of his or her possessions and income to the People's Temple. To leave would mean to abandon all the possessions they had, leaving them penniless and homeless. Staying could easily be justified, and the consequences seem more appealing than what could be faced outside.

The individual's isolation from any outside forces meant that even when they disagreed with the teachings or actions of the group, that disagreement was nowhere confirmed. With no support or agreement from another source, the individual would soon repress his own reservations. This process was made doubly effective, as each person was required to report any expressions of disagreement or dissatisfaction to Jones. Children would report their parents, husbands their wives, and parents their own children. It was not safe to trust anyone with your negative feelings, to do so would risk the public humiliation and severe punishments meted out for such "offences."

At "Jonestown" this isolation was even more extreme. The community was situated in the middle of a jungle with armed guards along the few roads that led to civilization. Even if one succeeded in leaving the complex, he had no passport, papers or money to help him to escape. When Ryan and his delegation arrived at "Jonestown," anyone who wanted to leave had the option of doing so openly without the normal threats to their safety, yet only fifteen chose to do so. This is a strong indication of the effectiveness of Jones's indoctrination.

And They Called Him 'Father'

Jim Jones was born in Lyn, Indiana in 1931 during the Great Depression. As his parents struggled to eke out an existence, Jones was free to explore the world around him. At an early age he happened upon a Pentecostal congregation known as the Gospel Tabernacle, made up mainly of people who had moved to the area from Kentucky and Tennessee. The church and its members dwelt on the fringes of the community and were known as "holy-rollers" and "tongues people" by the more conservative community of Lyn.

Peoples Temple leader
Reverend Jim Jones

By his early teens, Jones was no longer interested in the normal activities of the other boys. He was much more interested in the emotional and religious fervor he found at the Gospel Tabernacle. Here he learned about spiritual healing and was soon receiving praise for his preaching. In 1947 at the age of sixteen, Jones was preaching on street corners in both black and white neighborhoods, sharing the wisdom and knowledge that he believed he possessed and was obliged to share with others. He believed in the brotherhood of man, regardless of social standing or race. His sympathies lay with the poor and the downtrodden.

Jones considered himself a leader among his peers and looked down upon the behavior of other boys his age that he considered frivolous and sinful. Yet, he strongly feared rejection and would retaliate angrily at any adverse criticism or disagreement that he saw as betrayal. An example of this was when his best friend chose to go home rather than comply with Jones's demands. As his friend walked away, Jones grabbed his father's gun and shot at the boy's fast retreating figure.

During his high school years, Jones first became interested in the lives of powerful and influential men, taking a special interest in Adolf Hitler and Joseph Stalin. By the time he met his future wife, Marceline, in his late teens, he had already developed a keen knowledge and concern for social issues and world events. Marceline was a student nurse at the hospital where Jones worked part-time. They married after Jones graduated from high school with honors and began college. The first years of their marriage were very stormy. Jones was insecure and domineering. His greatest fear that of being abandoned by the ones he cared about, caused him to be jealous of any attention Marceline gave to anyone else. Jones's constant emotional explosions and tirades were extremely difficult for Marceline, but her belief that marriage was a lifetime commitment caused her to endure.

Throughout this period, Jones began to question his faith, finding it difficult to reconcile his belief in a loving and merciful God with the reality of suffering and poverty he saw around him. He now proclaimed that there was no God. He expected Marceline to share his new wisdom and threatened to commit suicide if she continued to pray. He softened his view in 1952 when the Methodists, the denomination of the church that Marceline attended, displayed a social conscience in line with his own beliefs. The church espoused the rights of minorities and worked toward putting an end to poverty. The Methodists' opposition to unemployment and support for collective bargaining for workers and security for the aged particularly impressed Jones.

In the same year, while continuing his college studies, Jones accepted a position as student pastor at the Somerset Methodist Church in a less affluent, mostly white neighborhood in southern Indianapolis. Secretly, Jones visited a number of African-American churches in the area and invited those he met there to his own services and into his home. During this time Jones attempted to adopt Marceline's cousin, who had been living with them since they rescued him from a foster home. The twelve-year-old boy was not happy about this decision and resisted. Jones told him that any thought of returning to his mother was hopeless as she was unfit and didn't love him. After visiting his mother, the boy believed differently. In an emotional rage, Jones attempted to impose his will upon the boy, but he would not be swayed. He returned to live with his mother and refused to see Jones when he came to visit.

Within a couple of years, Jones was successfully preaching at Pentecostal meetings at other churches, drawing large crowds with his healings and miracles. This success led him to leave The Somerset Methodist Church and begin his own church. By 1956, he moved his congregation to larger premises and began calling his activities a "movement" and his church the "People's Temple." His emotional style and preaching of integration and equality were unusual qualities in a white preacher in the mid-fifties and Jones's congregation did not provide the strong financial backing needed to increase his influence. Despite its lack of numbers, Jones's church established a soup kitchen and advocated giving shelter to the needy and the adoption of children. At this time, Jones and Marceline adopted a black child and a Korean orphan as well as giving birth to a son.

The intensity of the Cold War in the mid-fifties influenced Jones considerably and he believed that Communism could best be fought with communalism. He was able to Christianize his burgeoning political beliefs by referring to biblical passages about people selling their possessions. Jones's good works and belief in civil rights was soon rewarded by his appointment as head of the Indianapolis Human Rights Commission. His radical beliefs and actions at this time brought many complaints and criticisms from the conservative sectors of the community. Jones began to relate to local newspapers stories of harassment and threats to his life, although none of his claims could be substantiated by police inquiries.

Coincidentally, it was as criticism of his politics was heightening that Jones had a "vision" of nuclear attack. Believing that the Midwest was the most likely target of such an attack, Jones began looking for a "safer" place to move his congregation. Leaving his congregation in the hands of his assistants, Jones went in search of the ideal location. He travelled to Hawaii and then Brazil where he stayed for two years, teaching English to support himself. It was during his return trip from Brazil that Jones first visited Guyana where he was impressed by the socialist doctrines of the government.

In 1965, two years after his return to Indianapolis, Jones moved with 140 of his followers to Ukiah in Mendocino County, California, because he had read in *Esquire* magazine that the area would be safe in the event of a nuclear attack. Once they were settled, Jones found part-time work as a teacher and Marceline worked as a social worker at Mendocino State hospital.

They had not been there long before Marceline decided she wanted to end their marriage. Jones's extra-marital sexual encounters had become more frequent since the move to California and his lust for power and control had increased dramatically. Their son Stephan had little respect for his father because of his hypocrisy. He made rules to satisfy his own whims, yet lived up to none of them himself. Jones was using a variety of drugs to control his emotional ups and downs including Quaaludes, which Stephan used to try to kill himself.

In 1968, with his family falling apart and his congregation only numbering 68, Jones applied for, and was granted, affiliation with the Disciples of Christ, a denomination that boasted 1.5 million members. With very little supervision from the church administration, Jones was able to ignore its requirement for Holy Communion and baptism; instead he preached socialism and baptized new members "in the holy name of socialism."

Being a member of a recognized church gave Jones tax exemptions and higher esteem. His congregation quickly grew to 300. Jones and his followers spent much of their time promoting the church and its good works, not only in the community but also across the country. Over 30,000 copies of a newsletter were sent nationwide every month and Jones began radio broadcasting, ensuring that his good works would be known by all. By 1973, his congregation had grown to two and a half thousand and had spread to San Francisco and Los Angeles where he began to preach as well.

In 1974, Jones obtained permission from the government of Guyana to begin building a commune on a 300-acre allotment, 140 miles from Georgetown. The lease was signed and Jones named the commune "Jonestown". With some of his followers already living at the commune site, Jones decided to visit Georgetown and publicize himself there. Members of his staff approached Father Andrew Morrison to gain permission for Jones to give a service at the Catholic Sacred Church. Ill-informed of the nature of Jones's preaching, Father Morrison and others who attended were horrified by the obviously fake healings and miracles that occurred.

Disappointed, Jones returned to California where the reception for his staged antics was much more favorable. Staff members, usually intellectuals with a strong mystical bent, would pilfer the garbage of temple members to glean information Jones could use to fake clairvoyance in his meetings. Potential Temple members were invited to small meetings where they were carefully screened. Anyone who appeared to be too politically conservative was excluded from further involvement, while those with anti-establishment attitudes and sympathy with Pentecostal type services were welcomed. These criteria meant that the majority of recruits were African-American, the uneducated and the poor.

In response to Jones's teaching of Christian communalism, Temple members pooled their incomes and turned their property over to the People's Temple to be sold, in return they received room, board and a two-dollar a week allowance. Jones preached that only through socialism could anyone achieve perfect freedom, justice and equality. According to Jones, socialism was the manifestation of God. His miracles, healing of the sick and care for the poor were all proof that he was Christ incarnate.

Jones saw himself as a social revolutionary despite the fact that his own organisation was anything but socialistic. There was no collective leadership and his staff, nearly all white, was not able to question his ideas. There was one source of authority only - Jim Jones.

Jones's dualism and hypocrisy were reflected in his teachings on sexual relationships. He believed in sexual liberation yet advocated marriage. He attacked marriage without sexual freedom as being counter-revolutionary; any spouse who reacted jealously over their partner's sexual infidelity was attacked openly. At the same time he preached the virtues of celibacy and the sexuality of all members were under attack. Each person was required to confess their sexual practices and fantasies, while women were required to publicly complain about their husbands' lovemaking. Jones told his congregation that he was the only true heterosexual, yet in private he sodomised a man, justifying his actions as being the only way to prove to that man that he was really homosexual. In December 1973, Jones was arrested in MacArthur Park, a known meeting place for homosexuals, and booked for lewd conduct. Although the charges were dismissed, Jones was required to sign a document admitting that there was good reason for the arrest.

Jones was able to keep his arrest a secret and continued to gain acceptance in the San Francisco area. Left-wing groups welcomed him for his support of progressive causes and anti-establishment teachings. Temple members worked in political campaigns in San Francisco and Jones cultivated relationships with a variety of powerful political figures, using his large congregation and large accumulation of People's Temple funds to cement his influence.

While his outside influence was growing and his control over his congregation was almost unbroken, Jones was not able to prevent all negative criticism directed at the People's Temple, although he did attempt to do so. He had members of his congregation take jobs in some of the leading newspapers in the area to warn him of any plans to print negative material about him. Before the papers could take the story to print, Jones would begin threatening them with legal action. Any of his opponents who persisted in discrediting him would soon receive threatening mail and be awoken in the middle of the night with threatening phone calls. Defectors from the Temple were too terrified to tell of their negative experiences with Jones, as they were constantly threatened with grave punishments.

Having been well experienced in Jones's punishments and his uncontrollable anger towards anyone who dared to leave him, defectors believed that he would make good his threats if they pushed him. Grace Stoen, the wife of Tim Stoen who was the Temple's Lawyer, experienced firsthand Jones's wrath when she dared to leave the community because of the brutal beating of a member who had criticized Jones. Jones was outraged at her betrayal in light of "all that he had done for her." With Tim's support, Jones began a fierce custody battle for the Stoens's son, whom Jones falsely claimed was his own.

It was this custody battle, along with a growing number of complaints from ex-members and relatives of members, which caused a great deal of public attention to become focused on the People's Temple. With the mounting negative publicity, Jones's paranoia became even more exaggerated and he began to prepare his congregation for the final move to Guyana.

Once in Guyana, Jones was able to maintain control over his community of followers without the conflicting input of outside agencies. Confined to the 300-acre property with no money or passports, Jones was guaranteed that no more of his followers could abandon him. He could now be in complete control of his people. When that control was again threatened by the departure of fifteen more people with Leo Ryan's party, Jones's vengeful act of murder at the airport was typical of Jones throughout his life. The order for the mass-suicide was his means to gain ultimate control, if he could not have control of his people in life, he would have it in death!

Sinister Connections?

Although the official explanation of the events at "Jonestown" has been widely accepted by the American people, there are many that question its truth. From the moment the first reports of the massacre were released, various theories of the real events leading to the tragedy began to circulate. The most prevalent of these was that the CIA was somehow involved.

Jim Jones (shades) greets San Francisco Mayor Moscone, who was assassinated one week after the Jonestown massacre.

The Reverend Jim Jones and San Francisco Mayor Moscone, who was murdered after the 'Jonestown' massacre.

According to one of these theories, "Jonestown" was a continuation of a CIA mind-control program that infiltrated cults, such as The People's Temple, to carry out their experiments. CIA theorists claim that Jim Jones had many questionable associations with the CIA throughout the years he was establishing The People's Temple. The most significant association is Jones's supposed friendship with

Dan Mitrione that dated back to their childhood years. Dan Mitrione was the local police chief in the early days of Jones's "ministry" in Indianapolis. Mitrione later entered the International Police Academy, supposedly a CIA front for training in counterinsurgency and torture techniques.

Coincidentally, when Jones left with his wife to live in Brazil, despite his apparent lack of financial resources, Mitrione was already living there. Jones is purported to have made several visits to Belo Horizonte where the CIA's Brazilian headquarters was situated and Mitrione resided. CIA theorists report that Jones's neighbours in Brazil state that Jones had told them that he was employed by the US Office of Naval Intelligence who supplied him with transport, living expenses and a large home in which he "lived like a rich man."

Soon after his return to America, with $10,000, Jones moved the People's Temple to California. Here he began building the People's Temple communal facilities and, without any trained medical personnel or the usual licensing, was able to run a nursing home. During this time Jones allegedly adopted 150 foster children, most of whom were sent to the People's Temple by court order. The Temple had a strong association with the World Vision organisation that many conspiracy theorists believe to be another CIA front, and had as a consultant, a mercenary from the rebel army UNITA, supposedly backed by the CIA.

Other supposed CIA connections with "Jonestown" include the allegations that:

Richard Dwyer's name had appeared in the publication *Who's Who In The CIA*

US Ambassador John Burke and another embassy official, Richard McCoy, had strong links with the CIA

The Georgetown CIA station was situated in the US Embassy building

Dan Webber, sent to Guyana immediately after the massacre, was with the CIA and

Joseph Blatchford, the officially appointed attorney for the "Jonestown" survivors, was involved in a scandal involving CIA infiltration of the Peace Corps.

The involvement of Larry Layton in the ambush of Ryan and his party also provokes great interest from the CIA theorists because of his family background. Layton's father was Dr. Laurence Laird Layton who had been the chief of the army's Chemical Warfare Division during the 1950's. It had also been Larry Layton's brother-in-law, the UNITA link, who had negotiated with the Guyana government, on behalf of Jones, for the establishment of "Jonestown."

Another point, which CIA theorists use to support their beliefs, is the fact that, despite the growing controversy surrounding the People's Temple, Jones's move to "Jonestown" was given full support from the American Embassy in Guyana.

Leo Ryan's murder is seen by many as being much more sinister than the hysterical behavior of a madman. Leo Ryan had been a strong critic of the CIA and was the author of the Hughes-Ryan Amendment, which, if passed, would have required that the CIA report to Congress on all of its covert operations before they commenced. Soon after Ryan's death, the Hughes-Ryan Amendment was quashed in Congress. The question conspiracy theorists ask is whether Ryan was killed in order to reach this objective and the massacre at "Jonestown" merely a smoke screen to distract attention away from Ryan's murder?

Witnesses at the airport, where Ryan and four others were murdered, described the gunmen as being "glassy eyed", "mechanically-walking zombies" who were "devoid of emotion." The question CIA theorists would like answered is who were these people? The official report stated that there were approximately 1100 people at "Jonestown" at the time of the massacre but other reports claim that there were closer to 1200. Of this number there were 913 dead bodies found and 167 survivors. Twenty people, if the 1100 figure is correct, are left unaccounted for. If they were the assassins, where are they now? Also unaccounted for, and never referred to in news reports, are the armed guards who were present in "Jonestown" but were free to come and go from the compound. A congressional aide may have been referring to these men in an Associated Press quote "There are 120 white, brainwashed assassins out from Jonestown, awaiting the trigger word to pick up their hit."

Such a possibility seems to be confirmed for the theorists by a number of unusual deaths that have occurred since the "Jonestown" massacre. The first of these occurred in Georgetown at the People's Temple headquarters at the same time as the "Jonestown" massacre. Charles Beikman, an early Jim Jones follower who had become an "adopted son" was found to be responsible. Apparently, Beikman was also a Green Beret, of which there were over 300 in Guyana at the time on a "training exercise."

Nine days after "Jonestown," San Francisco Mayor George Moscone and Supervisor Harvey Milk were killed. Both men had received financial support from Jones while he was in San Francisco and were involved in an ongoing investigation into their involvement in the disappearance of People's Temple funds. Dan White, described as being in a "zombie state" at the time of the killings, murdered them. White's lawyers attempted to defend their client by stating that White had been temporarily insane due to the effects of eating too much sugar, a defence which was mockingly known as the "Twinkie defence."

Sometime later, Michael Prokes, a former member of the People's Temple, informed a press conference, held in his motel room, that the CIA and FBI were secretly holding an audiotape of the "Jonestown" massacre and that he was an FBI informant. Immediately following his announcement, Prokes went into the bathroom where he supposedly committed suicide.

Jeanne and Alan Mills, People's Temple members who had defected before the move to Guyana, were found bound and killed in their home almost a year after the "Jonestown" massacre. They had written a book about the People's Temple and had expressed their belief that they would eventually be murdered. Official reports state that the Mills probably knew their murderers, as there were no signs of forced entry or struggle. Their son was at home at the time of the murders but somehow escaped death. The case continues to remain unsolved.

The final area of concern in the "Jonestown" massacre regards the official US decision not to conduct autopsies on the victims of the massacre; the reason given was that the cause of death was readily apparent. The results of pathology examinations conducted by Guyanese coroner Leslie Mootoo however, revealed his belief that as many as 700 of the victims were murders, not suicides. Mootoo claims that in a 32-hour period he, and his assistants, examined the bodies of 137 victims. They had all been injected with cyanide in areas of their bodies, which could not have been reached by their own hand, such as between the shoulder blades; many other victims had been shot. Charles Huff, one of the seven Green Berets who were the first American troops on the scene following the massacre, claimed that "We saw *many* bullet wounds as well as wounds from crossbow bolts." Those who were shot appeared to have been running toward the jungle, away from the compound, at the time they were shot.

The discrepancy in the numbers of dead in the first reports, and the final figure had led many to speculate that approximately five hundred people had escaped the first spate of killings and escaped into the jungle, but were then hunted down and murdered. The descriptions of witnesses to the layout of the bodies, and the fact that there were obvious signs that many of the bodies had been dragged to their final resting place, tends to contradict the 'official' explanation that at the first counting five hundred bodies had been concealed by the other 408 bodies.

Epilogue

Twenty-one years have passed since the tragedy of "Jonestown" occurred and still many wonder at how it came about. For many, the possibility that one man could manipulate so many people to such a great extent is incomprehensible. They look to a variety of sources to explain the apparently unexplainable, in a vain attempt to satisfy the need for understanding. Unfortunately, the processes that had been at work in the People's Temple for many years, ultimately leading to the mass suicide and murders of 913 of its members, are not unique to this particular group. We are social creatures who need to feel that we belong to something greater than ourselves and rely heavily upon the approval of others to measure our worth. Such a situation leaves us vulnerable to others, quickly changing our viewpoints to fit in with those around us, denying our own instinctive values and beliefs when faced with the conflicting views of others. People such as Jim Jones, driven by their own insatiable need to be accepted and loved, have an instinctive knowledge of the weaknesses of others and how to manipulate them to their own advantage.

Whether "Jonestown" was the result of some heinous experiment in mind control or not, cannot be fully determined one way or the other without stronger evidence, but the cloud of mystery will continue to hang over the incident until all of the documentation collected during the investigations have been revealed. At the time that it released its report, the US State Department chose to withhold over 8000 documents pertaining to "Jonestown" for a number of years. After many legal battles, it was determined that these documents should be released.

Perhaps, as the information in these documents becomes available some of the mystery will be solved.

CHARLES MANSON

Quiet and secluded is just what the young movie star wanted. The canyons above Beverly Hills were far enough away from the noisy glitz of Hollywood to afford some privacy and space. Sharon Tate loved this place on Cielo Drive. To her it meant romance — romance with the man of her dreams and the father of her child, director Roman Polanski.

Charles Manson

It was cooler up there too, which was especially refreshing on that hot muggy Saturday night, the 9th of August 1969. The beautiful young woman kept herself company with her attractive and sophisticated friends: Abigail Folger, the coffee heiress and her boyfriend Voytek Frykowski, and an internationally known hair stylist Jay Sebring.

Sharon was eight months pregnant and very lonely for her husband who was away in Europe working on a film.

Impromptu gatherings like this one on a weekend night were not at all unusual.

The house was deliberately secluded but not completely insecure. Approximately 100 feet from the house was a locked gate and on the property was a guesthouse inhabited by an able-bodied young caretaker.

That night the Kotts, Sharon's nearest neighbors who lived about 100 yards away, thought they heard a few gunshots coming from the direction of Sharon's property sometime between 12:30 and 1 A.M. But since they heard nothing else, they went to bed.

Around the same time, a man supervising a camp-out less than a mile away heard a chilling scream: "Oh, God, no, please don't! Oh, God, no, don't, don't..."

He drove around the area, but found nothing unusual.

Nearby a neighbor's dogs went into a barking frenzy somewhere between 2 and 3 A.M. He got out of bed and looked around, but found nothing amiss and went back to bed.

A private security guard hired by some of the wealthy property owners thought he heard several gunshots a little after 4 A.M. and called his headquarters. Headquarters, in turn, called Los Angeles Police Department to report the disturbance. The LAPD officer said: "I hope we don't have a murder; we just had a woman-screaming call in that area."

The Tate/Polanski House on Cielo Drive

Winifred Chapman, Sharon Tate's housekeeper, got to the main gate of the house a little after 8 A.M. She noticed what looked like a fallen telephone wire hanging over the gate. She pushed the gate control mechanism and it swung open. As she walked up to the house, she saw an unfamiliar white Rambler parked in the driveway.

When she got to the house, she took the house key from its hiding place and unlocked the back door. Once inside the kitchen, she picked up the telephone and confirmed that it was a telephone wire that had fallen, completely knocking out all phone service. As she made her way toward the living room, she noticed that the front door was open and that there were splashes of red everywhere. Looking out the front door, she saw a couple of pools of blood and what appeared to be a body on the lawn.

She shrieked and ran back through the house and down the driveway, passing close enough to the Rambler to see that there was yet another body inside the car. She ran over to the Kotts and banged on the door, but they were not home, so she ran to the next house and did the same thing, screaming hysterically.

The Crime Scene

10050 Cielo Drive

Victims: Sharon Tate, Jay Sebring, Abigail Folger, Voytek
Frykowski and Steve Parent

LAPD Officer Jerry DeRosa arrived first. He walked up to
the Rambler and found a young man slumped toward the
passenger side, drenched in blood.

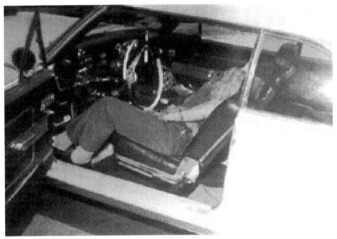
Steve Parent

At this point, Officer William Whisenhunt joined DeRosa. The two officers, with guns drawn searched the other automobiles and the garage, while a third officer Robert Burbridge caught up with them.

There on the beautifully manicured lawn with its magnificent panorama of Los Angeles lay two bodies. One was a white man that appeared to be in his thirties. Someone had battered in his head and face, while savagely puncturing the rest of his body with dozens of wounds.

Voytek Frykowski

The other body was that of a young woman with long brown hair lying in a full-length nightgown with multiple stab wounds.

Abigail Folger

The three officers cautiously approached the house. No telling what or who may be waiting in there for them. It would have been foolhardy for all of them to enter through the front door. However, as they went near the front door, they saw that one of the front window screens had been removed. Whisenhunt found an open window on the side of the house where he and Burbridge made their entry.

Once the other two officers were inside, DeRosa approached the front door. On the lower half of the door, he saw scrawled in blood the word "PIG."

In the hallway they found two large steamer trunks, a pair of horned rimmed glasses and pieces of a broken gun grip.

Then when they reached the couch, they were in for a real shock. A young blond woman, very pregnant, was laying on the floor, smeared all over with blood, a rope around her neck that extended over a rafter in the ceiling. The other end of the rope was around the neck of a man lying nearby, also drenched in blood.

Sharon Tate and Jay Sebring

As they looked through the rest of the house they heard a man's voice and the sound of a dog. It was William Garretson the caretaker. The officers handcuffed him and put him under arrest.

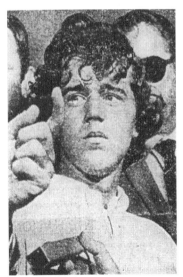

William Garretson

The photo with Roman Polanski as it appeared in Life
magazine in 1969

The bodies of the victims being removed from the house

3301 Waverly Drive

Victims: Leno and Rosemary LaBianca

Later that Saturday night, Leno and Rosemary LaBianca and Susan Struthers, Rosemary's 21-year-old daughter, drove back from vacation trailering their boat. They dropped off Susan at her apartment and drove home to 3301 Waverly Drive in the Los Feliz area of L.A. They stopped to pick up a newspaper between 1 and 2 A.M.

3301 Waverly Drive

It wasn't until the next day that anybody came to the house to see them.   Frank Struthers, Rosemary's son by a previous marriage, got a ride home.   Around 8:30 P.M., as he carried his camping equipment up the driveway, he noticed things that worried him.   First the speedboat was still in the driveway.   It was very unlike his stepfather not to put the boat in the garage.   Then Frank noticed that all the window shades were down — something his parents never did.

He knocked on the door, but got no answer, so he went to a pay phone and called, but again with no response. He finally got in touch with his sister, who came with her boyfriend to their parents' house.

Frank and the boyfriend found the back door open. They left Susan in the kitchen until they had a chance to look around. When the two young men walked into the living room, they saw Leno in his pajamas, lying with a pillow over his head and a cord around his neck. Something was sticking out from his stomach.

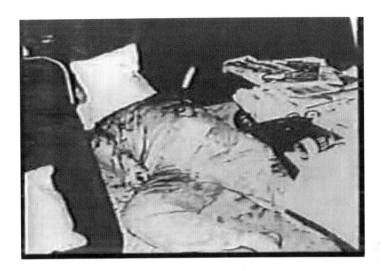

They rushed out of the house, dragging Susan with them and called the police at the neighbors' house.

Soon an ambulance and police cars arrived. Leno was found with a blood-drenched pillowcase over his head and the cord of a large lamp tied tightly around his neck. His hands had been tied behind him with a leather thong. A carving fork protruded from his stomach and the word "WAR" had been carved in his flesh.

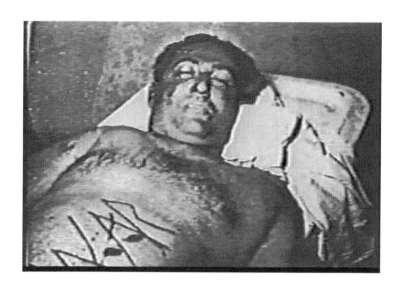

In the master bedroom, they found his wife Rosemary lying on the floor, her nightgown up over her head. She too had a pillowcase over her head and a lamp cord tied tightly around her neck.

In three places in the house, there was writing which appeared to be in the victims' blood: on the living room wall, "DEATH TO PIGS;" on another wall in the living room, the single word "RISE;" and in the refrigerator door, "HEALTHER SKELTER," misspelled.

The Slaughtered - Sharon Tate

Eventually, all of the victims of the massacre at Sharon Tate's home were identified. The young man in the car was a teenager named Steve Parent who had come to visit Garretson, the caretaker. The two victims found outside the house were Abigail Folger and her lover, Voytek Frykowski. In the living room joined by rope were Sharon Tate and Jay Sebring.

A .22 caliber gun had shot Steve Parent, Jay Sebring and Voytek Frykowski. Of the five victims, all but Steve Parent had been stabbed repeatedly. Sebring had been hit in the face and Frykowski had been repeatedly hit on the head with a blunt object.

The stab wounds suggested that only one knife had been used for the wounds. The nature of the wounds indicated that something like a bayonet was the weapon. A strange knife, a Buck brand clasp-type pocketknife that the housekeeper could not identify was found very close to Sharon Tate's body.

Sharon Tate

Sharon Tate had been a beauty all of her life. Even as a child she had won beauty contests. But her ambition was not to be a model but a movie actress. Finally in 1963 at the age of 22 she found a sponsor in Producer Martin Ransohoff. With Ransohoff's help, she landed parts in the series *Beverly Hillbillies* and *Petticoat Junction,* and the movies *The Americanization of Emily* and *The Sandpiper.*

In 1965, she got her chance at her first feature role in the Eye of the Devil with David Niven and Deborah Kerr. In this movie she played the part of a country girl with special magical powers. While in London in the summer of 1966 for the filming of the movie, she met Roman Polanski, who had just made his mark as a director of the movie Repulsion with Catherine Deneuve and Cul de Sac, which had won many European film awards.

Polanski put Sharon as the lead in his campy film The Fearless Vampire Killers. During this period she became Polanski's lover. This relationship lasted quite a long time and shortly after the filming of Rosemary's Baby, he and Sharon married. In 1969, they rented the house on Cielo Drive from Terry Melcher, Doris Day's son and moved in mid-February.

Sharon's career never skyrocketed the way Polanski's did even with her role as Jennifer in Valley of the Dolls. A good part of the reason her career was going nowhere is that she never had an opportunity to show off whatever acting skills she had. All the roles she had were ones in which all she had to do was look pretty. Her career took a backseat when she became pregnant. The baby and her husband became the center of her life.

She was a unique lady according to most everyone who knew her. In spite of her beauty and remarkable figure, she was a very down-to-earth woman with none of the phoniness normally associated with starlets. She was very sweet and a bit on the naïve side. Everyone seemed to like Sharon even in a jealous, bitchy town like Hollywood.

Sharon's life was ended by five stab wounds in her chest and back, which penetrated her heart, lungs and liver and caused massive internal hemorrhaging. The remaining eleven wounds simply added insult to her savaged body.

Her little boy, Paul Richard Polanski, died with her.

Abigail & Her Lover

Abigail Folger, Sharon's friend was twenty-five years old when she died. As heiress to the Folger coffee fortune, she had led a very comfortable life. She made her debut in San Francisco in 1961. She graduated from Radcliffe. Like many wealthy girls, she looked for something meaningful to do with her time and became very involved in social work.

Folger and Frykowski

In 1968, she met her lover Voytek Frykowski who introduced her to Sharon and Roman Polanski. She became an investor in Jay Sebring's men's toiletries and hair styling business.

Her social work in the ghettos of Los Angeles was beginning to get to her.

She started to feel that her contribution was futile in combatting the enormous problems of ignorance and poverty. She told her friends that she couldn't get away from her work at the end of the day. "The suffering gets under your skin," she said.

Her relationship with Frykowski was also a source of concern to her. The two of them had become much too dependent upon drugs. Both the frustrations of her social work and her problems with Voytek were the subject of her almost daily conversations with a psychiatrist. She had just about built up enough strength to break off her love affair and try to get her life back on track when twenty-eight stab wounds intervened.

Voytek Frykowski was thirty-two when he died. He had been a long-time friend of Roman's from Poland. He was, according to Polanski, "a man of little talent but immense charm." Always a playboy, he had no visible means of support, essentially living off Abigail's money. While he told people he was a writer, there was no evidence that he was anything but a very charming, extroverted and entertaining "druggie."

However dissipated his life was or charming his personality, it came to an abrupt end with two gunshot wounds, thirteen blows to the head and fifty-one stab wounds.

Jay Sebring

Jay Sebring

Jay Sebring was quite the opposite career-wise from Frykowski. He was the top men's hairstylist in the U.S. and was a major force in the development of a market for men's hair products and toiletries. His customers included Frank Sinatra, Peter Lawford, George Peppard, Paul Newman and Steve McQueen. His new company, Sebring International would franchise men's hair styling shops and his line of hair products.

He was known as a ladies man and dated many different women. One of those women had at one time been Sharon

Tate, who broke off her relationship with Sebring when she became involved with Polanski.

There was another, darker side to Sebring's exuberant sex life. He would tie up his girlfriends and occasionally whip them before they had sex. In spite of his flashy, successful outward life, there was reason to suspect that the real Jay Sebring was lonely and insecure.

A gunshot wound and seven stab wounds liberated him from his insecurities.

More Victims

Steven Parent

Aside from Sharon Tate's baby, the youngest victim was 18-year-old Steven Earl Parent who lived with his father, mother and siblings in El Monte. At around 11:45 P.M. Saturday night, Parent had come onto the estate to visit William Garretson, the caretaker who was living in the guesthouse. Parent's hobby was hi-fi equipment and he wanted to show Garretson a radio he brought with him. Garretson wasn't interested and Parent left the guesthouse around 12:15 A.M.

The young man had just graduated from high school in June and worked several jobs so that he could go to college in the fall.

Instead he got four bullets from a .22 caliber revolver.

Leno LaBianca

Leno LaBianca was a respectable businessman. His father was the founder of State Wholesale Grocery Company and Leno went into the family business right out of college. He was a man who was well liked and did not appear to have any enemies. People described him as a quiet, conservative person.

He died from the multiple stab wounds, twenty-six in all.

Rosemary LaBianca

Rosemary LaBianca was an attractive 38-year-old woman of Mexican origin. She had been orphaned as a child and later adopted when she was twelve. She had worked as a carhop and a waitress. She met her first husband in the 1940's and had two children. After they were divorced in 1958, she met Leno when she was a waitress at the Los Feliz Inn.

Rosemary had become a very successful businesswoman. Not only did she run the profitable Boutique Carriage, but also her prudent investments in securities and commodities left her with an estate of $2.6 million. Not bad for someone who started life with no advantages and spent most of her career as a waitress and carhop.

She had been stabbed forty-one times, six of which were enough to have caused her death.

On two consecutive nights, seven innocent adults and one unborn child lost their lives in what seemed to be a senseless, motiveless crime.

However one feels about the lifestyles of the wealthy and glamorous, it is hard to imagine any social good coming from these vicious murders. Yet over the years, the perpetrators of these crimes and their persistent followers have tried to suggest that these killings were necessary and desirable.

This author hopes that nobody finishing this story will agree.

Suspicion

In his very thorough book on the case, *Helter Skelter*,
Prosecutor Vincent Bugliosi heaps a great deal of fault
upon the homicide detectives of the Los Angeles Police
Department. One of the examples he provides is the
LAPD's slowness to connect the Tate murders with the
LaBianca murders the following night and with the murder
of Gary Hinman a few days earlier. Some of this fault on
the part of the LAPD apparently stemmed from its lack of
cooperation with the Los Angeles County Sheriff's Office.

Victim Gary Hinman

The LAPD was approached shortly after the Tate-LaBianca
murders by two LA Sheriff's Office detectives who told
them of the July 31 murder of music teacher Gary Hinman.
On the wall of the dead man's living room was written in

his own blood "POLITICAL PIGGY," which seemed very similar to the words written at both the Tate and the LaBianca crimes scenes. Also, Hinman had been stabbed to death as had victims at the Tate and LaBianca homes.

Amazingly enough, the LAPD detectives refused to examine any connection between the deaths of Hinman and the people at the Tate house. Furthermore, the LaBianca murders were squarely in the territory of the LA Sheriff's Office and the LAPD had no interest.

Bobby Beausoleil

Had the LAPD detectives bothered to listen to the LA Sheriff's Office detectives, they would have heard that the Sheriff's Office had arrested a Bobby Beausoleil for the Hinman murder. A Beausoleil who had been living with a bunch of hippies led by Charles Manson. But, the LAPD had already decided that the Tate murders were a result of a drug deal gone bad and didn't want to hear about any hippies.

On the other hand, the LAPD had in custody one William Garretson, the caretaker on the Tate estate who claimed that he slept through the entire bloody ordeal. The case against the frightened young man never materialized after he passed a polygraph test.

Officials essentially discounted robbery as a motive for the crimes, even though Rosemary LaBianca's wallet and wristwatch were missing. In the two homes of these affluent victims there were many items of value, which had not been touched by the killers. Small amounts of cash lying around the Tate home were still in evidence and the purses and wallets of the Tate victims were intact.

The LAPD did investigate three alleged dope dealers that had once crashed a party at the Polanski's, but one by one the men were cleared of any involvement.

Likewise, Roman Polanski was interviewed for hours by the police and agreed to a polygraph examination. On August 15, he returned for the first time since the murders to the house on Cielo Drive, accompanied by psychic Peter Hurkos.

Polanski had been devastated by the loss of his wife and son and was enraged at the media circus that he walked into when he got back to the States. He lashed out at the newspapers for suggesting that he and his wife were Satanists, indulging in sex and drug orgies. "Sharon," he said, "was so sweet and so lovely that I didn't believe that people like that existed...She was beautiful without phoniness. She was fantastic. She loved me and the last few years I spent with her were the only time of true happiness in my life..."

He worried to the police that perhaps he was the target not Sharon. "It could be some kind of jealousy or plot or something. It couldn't be Sharon directly." Polanski did not believe that drugs were a motive for the crimes. His wife, although she had experimented with LSD before they met, was not a big drug user. "I can tell you without question," he told the police. "She took no drugs at all, except for pot, and not too much of that. And during her pregnancy there was no question, she was so in love with her pregnancy she would do nothing. I'd pour a glass of wine and she wouldn't touch it."

The Reward

One month after the murders, Polanski, along with other contributors such as Peter Sellers, Yul Brynner and Warren Beatty, put an ad in the LA area newspapers for a reward:

REWARD

$25,000

Roman Polanski and friends of the Polanski family offer to pay a $25,000 reward to the person or persons who furnish information leading to the arrest and conviction of the murderer or murderers of Sharon Tate, her unborn child, and the other four victims.

It seemed like it was open season on theories. Everybody had a theory. The Mafia did it, the Polish secret police, etc. Sharon's father, Colonel Paul Tate, a former Army intelligence officer, launched his own private investigation. Letting his hair grow long and growing a beard, he started to frequent the hippie joints, the drug markets, hoping that he would get some tidbit of information that would lead to the murderers of his beloved daughter and grandson.

On September 1, 1969, a 10-year-old boy found a gun on his lawn in Sherman Oaks. He carefully took the .22 caliber Hi Standard Longhorn revolver to his father, who immediately called the LAPD. The gun was dirty and rusty and had a broken gun grip.

A couple of weeks earlier, the LAPD forensics experts determined that the .22 caliber revolver with the broken grip used on the Tate victims was none other than a Hi

Standard .22 caliber Longhorn revolver, which was relatively unique and rare. Amazingly enough, two weeks later, an identical gun with a broken grip is turned in to the LAPD, tagged, filed away and completely forgotten.

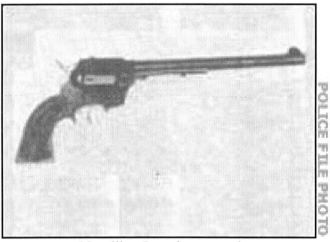

.22 caliber Longhorn revolver

A couple of days later, the LAPD sent out flyers to all personnel describing the murder gun and attaching a photo of the revolver. The flyer was also sent out to other law enforcement agencies around the country and Canada, while all the time, the gun sat in the Property Section of the Van Nuys division.

Three months after the murders, which had been separately pursued by the LAPD and the LA Sheriff's Office, neither group had made any progress. However, the detectives working for the Sheriff's Office were younger and more aggressive than their LAPD counterparts and came to the conclusion that the Tate and LaBianca cases were definitely connected. They had several suspects, one of which was Charles Manson.

The Spahn Ranch

The Spahn Ranch

Finally in mid-October, the LAPD began to talk to the Sheriff's Office and decided to investigate similarities between the murder of Gary Hinman and the Tate-LaBianca crimes. The investigation leads to the Spahn Ranch, which was the home of a hippie group that called itself the Manson Family.

The Spahn Ranch was in the mountains near Chatsworth. In the 1920's it had been the site for old cowboy movies. Author John Gilmore in his book *The Garbage People* describes the isolated old movie set:

The façade of the main street, a cluster of rundown movie buildings, had become a ghost town with its Longhorn

Saloon, the Rock City Café, some stables, weathered props and old trailers. Millions of moviegoers once viewed this old "Wild West" setting, but the dust had settled. Rusted car parts littered the grounds and few visitors passed by...

Bobby Beausoleil, the man charged with the murder of Gary Hinman, had lived at the Spahn Ranch with the Manson Family.

His 17-year-old girlfriend told police that Manson sent Bobby and a girl named Susan Atkins to Hinman's house to get money from him. When Hinman wouldn't give them the money, they killed him. She also recalled that Susan Atkins mentioned a fight with a man who she stabbed in the legs several times.

When police questioned Susan Atkins, who was still in jail, she admitted that she went with Beausoleil to Hinman's home to get some money he had inherited. When he refused, Beausoleil slashed his face. The two of them kept Hinman prisoner in his home until Beausoleil murdered him a couple of days later.

At that point there did not seem to be any direct connection between Beausoleil and the Tate-LaBianca murders, except for some hearsay that Susan Atkins had stabbed a man in the leg. Gary Hinman had not been stabbed in the leg, but Voytek Frykowski had.

Susan Atkins

Susan Atkins

While she was awaiting trial for the murder of Gary Hinman, Susan Atkins was placed in the Sybil Brand Institute, L.A.'s women's house of detention. Her bed was next to that of 31-year-old Ronnie Howard. Another inmate, Virginia Graham, was a close friend of Ronnie's. Susan Atkins was a real talker. She had an almost unbelievable story that Ronnie and Virginia listened to with absolute amazement.

Atkins acted like a nut case: dancing and singing at the oddest times, oblivious to the seriousness of the charges against her and bubbling over with laughter and delight without any apparent reason.

In the course of conversation, Susan told Virginia that she was in for first degree murder.

"Did you do it?" Virginia wanted to know.

"Sure," Susan answered as though it were the most natural response in the world. But, the police thought that she only held Hinman while Bob Beausoleil stabbed him. In reality, Susan said, it was she who stabbed Hinman while Beausoleil held him.

She also told Virginia that her lover Charlie was Jesus Christ and he was going to lead her to a hole in the earth in Death Valley where there was a civilization down there. After hearing that story, Virginia was convinced that Atkins was completely nuts.

Several days later on November 6, Susan was again in a talky mood and mentioned the Sharon Tate murder. "You know who did it don't you?"

Confession

Virginia said she didn't.

"Well, you're looking at her."

Virginia was horrified and asked why she did such a thing.

"Because we wanted to do a crime that would shock the world that the world would have to stand up and take notice."

Atkins went on to explain that they selected the Tate house because it was isolated. Susan said they knew who the owner was but they didn't know or care who would be at the house that night.

Susan explained that there were four of them, three girls and a man, all of whom had been given their instructions by Charlie. When they got to the gate, the man cut the telephone wires. Next they shot the teenager four times because he had seen them.

When they got in the house, Susan said that in the living room there was a man on the couch and a woman on the chair reading. Then some of Susan's group stayed in the living room, while Susan went into the bedroom where Sharon was sitting on the bed talking to Jay Sebring. They quickly put nooses over Sharon and Jay's heads so that if they moved they would choke.

Frykowski ran for the door. "He was full of blood," she said and claimed that she had stabbed him three or four times. "He was bleeding and he ran to the front part, and would you believe that he was there hollering 'Help, help, somebody please help me,' and nobody came? Then we finished him off."

"Sharon was the last to die," Susan said with a laugh as she described how Sharon was begging her, "Please don't kill me. Please don't kill me. I don't want to die. I want to live. I want to have my baby. I want to have my baby."

Susan said she just looked at Sharon straight in the eye and said, "Look, bitch, I don't care about you. I don't care if you're going to have a baby. You had better be ready. You're going to die and I don't feel anything about it...In a few minutes I killed her."

Susan said she saw that there was Sharon's blood on her hand and she tasted it. "Wow, what a trip! To taste death, and yet give life."

Flabbergasted, Virginia asked Susan if it didn't bother her to kill a pregnant woman.

"I thought you understood. I loved her, and in order for me to kill her I was killing part of myself when I killed her," Susan explained. She had wanted to cut out Sharon's baby but there wasn't enough time. She had also wanted to take out all the victims' eyes and squash them against the walls and cut off and mutilate all of their fingers, but they didn't have the chance.

Susan told Virginia that after they left the Tate house she realized that she didn't have her knife with her any more. Not only that, she had left her palm print on a desk, "but my spirit was so strong that obviously it didn't even show up or they would have me by now." The four of them drove to a place where they were able to wash their hands and change their clothes.

The Plan

Susan ended the story with admitting that they killed the LaBianca's the next night. "That's part of the plan," she explained. "And there's more."

This tale of murder had Virginia's head spinning. She told Ronnie Howard, who didn't believe the story. "She's making it all up. She could have gotten it out of the papers," Ronnie reasoned. Virginia came up with a way to test Susan about whether she was telling the truth.

Some years earlier when the Tate house had been up for lease, Virginia had actually been to see the exterior of the house on Cielo drive. When she saw Susan, she asked her if the house was still decorated in gold and white. Susan said no.

Virginia also picked up some miscellaneous pieces of information that tied Charlie and Susan to that house. It used to belong to Terry Melcher, Doris Day's son. Charlie and Susan were angry with Melcher for some reason that was not clear. She babbled something about Melcher being too interested in money.

Later that day, Susan began to talk again and gave Virginia the list of celebrity targets that were next on their list: Richard Burton and Elizabeth Taylor, Frank Sinatra, Steve McQueen and Tom Jones. It was important to select victims that would shock the world.

She had planned to carve the words "helter skelter" on Elizabeth Taylor's face with a red-hot knife and then gouge her eyes out. Then she would castrate Richard Burton and put his penis along with Elizabeth Taylor's eyes in a bottle and mail it to Eddie Fisher.

Sinatra was to be skinned alive, while he listened to his own music. The Family would then make purses out of his skin and sell them in hippie shops. Tom Jones would have his throat slit, but only after being forced to have sex with Susan Atkins.

More Confessions

People who knew them but were not part of the group reported other confessions from Manson and Family members about the same time. On November 12, the L.A. Sheriff's detectives had a chance to interview Al Springer who was a member of the motorcycle gang called the Straight Satans who had been involved with the Manson Family off and on.

The detectives were astonished when Springer told them that a few days after the Tate murders that Manson had bragged to him about killing people: "We knocked off five of them just the other night." Springer stayed clear of Manson after that, but mentioned that Danny DeCarlo, another member of the motorcycle gang lived at the Spahn Ranch with the Family.

Springer and DeCarlo

In the course of the interview Springer asked if anyone had their refrigerator wrote on? "Charlie said they wrote something on the fucking refrigerator in blood...Something about pigs or niggers or something like that."

When the police finally got to Danny DeCarlo, they really got an earful about Charlie and his Family. Not only did DeCarlo confirm their culpability in Gary Hinman's death, but he implicated them in the death of a 36-year-old ranch hand named Shorty, a nickname for Donald Shea. He was killed because he'd tell the owner of the Spahn Ranch what was really happening on his property. "Shorty was going to tell old man Spahn...and Charlie didn't like snitches," DeCarlo explained.

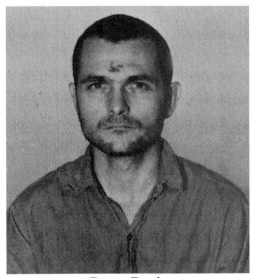
Bruce Davis

DeCarlo had been told what they did to his friend Shorty: "they stuck him like carving up a Christmas turkey...Bruce (Davis) said they cut him up in nine pieces. They cut his head off. Then they cut his arms off too, so there was no way they could possibly identify him. They were laughing about that."

Another Family member named Clem told DeCarlo with a big grin that "we got five piggies" the day after the Tate murders.

The two detectives shared this information with the detectives at the LAPD, but the latter did nothing with the information. The L.A. Sheriff's detectives, on the other hand, now focused their investigation on the Manson family believing that the hippie cult was somehow tied into both the Tate and LaBianca murder cases.

At some point in mid-November, Susan Atkins told her story to Ronnie Howard. Ronnie Howard felt that she had to tell the police about what Susan had revealed, especially since other people were future targets of the group. She asked for permission to contact LAPD, but was repeatedly denied, even though the woman she asked permission was dating one of the Tate case homicide detectives. Virginia Graham, who had been transferred to another facility, was running into the same kind of difficulty when she tried to tell the authorities about Susan.

Finally on November 17, 1969, two LAPD homicide detectives came to Sybil Brand to interview Ronnie Howard. The message was finally beginning to penetrate the collective intelligence of the LAPD that they had just found a gold mine. After they interviewed her, they had her moved for her safety into an isolation unit.

Charlie Manson

Just who was this Charlie anyway? Both the LAPD and the
Los Angeles Sheriff's Office started to dig through the
rubble of his heavily documented 36 years. As information
came in about him, it was no surprise that he was in
trouble. If ever a kid had a miserable start in life Charles
Manson was it.

Little Charles Manson with his cousin (and possibly grandmother).

An illegitimate and unplanned child, he was born in Cincinnati, Ohio, November 12, 1934 to Kathleen Maddox, a promiscuous sixteen-year-old who drank too much and got into a lot of trouble. Two years later, Kathleen filed suit against Colonel Scott of Ashland, KY, for child support, which she was awarded, but never received. Kathleen was briefly married to William Manson who gave his name to the boy.

Charles Manson in Nuel Emmons' book *Manson in His Own Words* describes the Maddox family:

Kathleen was the youngest of three children from the marriage of Nancy and Charles Maddox. Her parents loved her and meant well by her, but they were fanatical in their religious beliefs. Especially Grandma, who dominated the household. She was stern and unwavering in her interpretation of God's Will, and demanded that those within her home abide by her view of God's wishes.

My grandfather worked for the B&O Railroad. He worked long hard hours, a dedicated slave to the company and his bosses...He was not the disciplinarian Grandma was...If he tried to comfort Mom with a display of affection, such as a pat on the knee or an arm around her shoulder, Grandma was quick to insinuate he was vulgar.

For Mom, life was filled with a never-ending list of denials. From awakening in the morning until going to bed at night it was, "No Kathleen, that dress is too short. Braid your hair; don't comb it like some hussy. Come directly home from school; don't let me catch you talking to any boys. No, you can't go to the school dance; we are going to church..." In 1933, at age fifteen, my mother ran away from home.

Other writers have portrayed Mom as a teenage whore...In her search for acceptance she may have fallen in love too easily and too often, but a whore at that time? No!...In later years, because of hard knocks and tough times, she may have sold her body some...

Charlie never knew his father and never had a real father figure. His mother was the kind that children are taken away from and placed in foster homes. Kathleen had a habit of disappearing for days and weeks at a time, leaving Charlie with his grandmother or his aunt. When Kathleen and her brother were both sentenced to the penitentiary for armed robbery, Charlie got sent off to live with his aunt and uncle in McMechen, West Virginia. The aunt was very religious and strict in stark contrast to his mother's permissiveness.

When Kathleen was released from jail, she was not responsible enough to take care of him, preferring her life of promiscuity and hard drinking to any kind of normal lifestyle. There was no continuity in his life: he was always being foisted on someone new; he moved from one dingy rooming house to another; there were only transitory friendships that he made on the streets.

Manson Sold for a Pitcher of Beer

Manson tells the story that circulated within his family: "Mom was in a café one afternoon with me on her lap. The waitress, a would-be mother without a child of her own, jokingly told my Mom she'd buy me from her. Mom replied, 'A pitcher of beer and he's yours.' The waitress set up the beer; Mom stuck around long enough to finish it off and left the place without me. Several days later my uncle had to search the town for the waitress and take me home."

John Gilmore in his insightful book called *The Garbage People* describes how Charlie adapted to this life of emptiness and violence:

He kept to himself. Though friendless, his young mind bypassed the loneliness of his surroundings. He watched, listened, pretended his imaginative resources knew no limit. And he began to steal, as if to hold onto something that continually flew away. There was a consistency and permanency to the habit of stealing and it became easier. With everything transient, the thefts and goods he carried with him offered a sense of stability, a kind of reward. An object owned gave identity to an owner, an identity that had yet to be acknowledged.

Teen aged Charles Manson

When he was nine, he was caught stealing and sent to reform school and then later when he was twelve, he was caught stealing again and sent to the Gibault School for Boys in Terre Haute, Indiana, in 1947. He ran away less than a year later and tried to return to his mother who didn't want him. Living entirely by stealing and burglary, he lived on his own until he was caught. The court arranged for him to go to Father Flanagan's Boys Town.

He didn't last long at Boys Town. A few days after his arrival, thirteen-year-old Charlie and another kid committed two armed robberies. A few more episodes like that landed Charlie in the Indiana School for Boys for three years. His teachers described him as having trust in no one and "did good work only for those from whom he figured he could obtain something."

Institutional Politician

In 1951, Charlie and two other boys escaped and headed for California living entirely by burglary and auto theft. They got as far as Utah when they were caught. This time he was sent to the National Training School for Boys in Washington, D.C. While he was there they gave him various tests which established that his IQ was 109, that he was illiterate and that his aptitude for everything but music was average.

His keepers said this about him: "Manson has become somewhat of an 'institution politician.' He does just enough work to get by on. Restless and moody most of the time, the boy would rather spend his class time entertaining his friend. It appears that this boy is a very emotionally upset youth who is definitely in need of some psychiatric orientation."

That same year, Dr. Block, a psychiatrist examined him, noting "the marked degree of rejection, instability and psychic trauma." His illegitimacy, small physical size and lack of parental love caused him to constantly strive for status with the other boys. "This could add up to a fairly slick institutionalized youth," Dr. Block concluded, "but one is left with the feeling that behind all this lies an extremely sensitive boy who has not yet given up in terms of securing some kind of love and affection from the world."

For a short time, things started to look up for Charlie. His aunt had agreed to take care of him and his chances for parole were good. Shortly before the parole hearing, Charlie held a razor blade against another boy's throat while he sodomized him. Charlie was transferred to the Federal Reformatory at Petersburg, Virginia, where he was characterized as definitely homosexual, dangerous and safe only under supervision.

In September of 1952, he was sent to a more secure institution in Chillicothe, Ohio. His keepers there saw him as "criminally sophisticated despite his age and grossly unsuited for retention in an open reformatory type institution." For some reason, Manson suddenly changed his attitude. He was more cooperative and genuinely improved educationally so that he was able to read and understand basic math. This improvement leads to his parole in May of 1954 at the age of nineteen.

At first he lived with his aunt and uncle, then his mother for a short period of time. Early in 1955, he married a waitress who bore him a son, Charles Manson, Jr. Charlie worked at various low-paying jobs and augmented his income by stealing cars. One of them he took to Los Angeles with his then pregnant wife. Inevitably, he was caught again and eventually found his way to the prison at Terminal Island in San Pedro, California.

Charles Manson with his wife (Wedding Day)

1956 Mugshot

The Manipulator

His wife had the good sense to divorce him after he spent three years in jail. In 1958, he was released on parole. This time Manson took up a new occupation — pimping. He supplemented this income by getting money from an unattractive wealthy girl in Pasadena. In 1959, Manson was arrested on two federal charges: stealing a check from a mailbox and attempting to cash a U.S. Treasury check for $37.50

This time Manson was lucky, a young woman pretended she was pregnant and pleaded with the judge to keep him out of jail. The judge believed the story and had pity on him. While he sentenced Charlie to ten years, he then immediately placed him on probation. A couple of months later, he was arrested by the LAPD for stealing cars and using stolen credit cards, but the charges were dropped for lack of evidence.

Near the end of 1959, Manson conned a young woman out of $700 in savings to invest in his nonexistent company. To make matters worse, he got her pregnant and then drugged and raped her roommate. He fled to Texas but was arrested and put in prison to serve out his ten-year sentence. "If there ever was a man who demonstrated himself completely unfit for probation, he is it," the judge said. Eventually at the age of 26 he was sent to the U.S. Penitentiary at McNeil Island, Washington.

His record there described Charlie as having "a tremendous drive to call attention to himself. Generally he is unable to succeed in positive acts; therefore he often resorts to negative behavior to satisfy this drive. In his efforts to "find" himself, Manson peruses different religious philosophies, e.g. Scientology and Buddhism; however, he never remains long enough with any given teachings to reap meaningful benefits."

By 1964, he hadn't changed much, as least as viewed by prison officials: "His past pattern of employment instability continues...seems to have an intense need to call attention to himself...remains emotionally insecure and tends to involve himself in various fanatical interests."

Whatever those "fanatical" interests were, they included an obsession with the Beatles. Manson's guitar was another obsession. He felt that with the right opportunities he would be much bigger than the Beatles. In prison, he became friends with the aging gangster, Alvin Karpis. The former Public Enemy Number One and sole survivor of the Ma Barker gang taught Charlie how to play the steel guitar. The prison record noted in May of 1966 that "he has been spending most of his free time writing songs, accumulating about 80 or 90 of them during the past year...He also plays the guitar and drums, and is hopeful that he can secure employment as a guitar player or as a drummer or singer."

Karpis had some interesting insights into Charlie's true personality: "There was something unmistakably unusual about Manson. He was a runt of sorts, but found his place as an experienced manipulator of others. I did feel manipulated, and under circumstances where it hadn't been necessary."

On March 21, 1967, Charlie was released from prison and given transportation to San Francisco. He was 32 years old and more than half of his life had been spent in institutions. He protested his freedom. "Oh, no, I can't go outside there...I knew that I couldn't adjust to that world, not after all my life had been spent locked up and where my mind was free. I was content to stay in the penitentiary, just to take my walks around the yard in the sunshine and to play my guitar..." The prison officials ignored his protest and unleashed him on the world again.

Charlie's Followers
"The Manson Family"

As poorly prepared for life on the outside as he was, Charlie was able to blend in with his guitar into the hippie scene in San Francisco. The high-point of the Haight Ashbury culture was past and the only ones left were the diehards and the last ones to the party. Charlie was never impressed by the hippie culture, but he lived off it and it didn't expect much from him. He learned about drugs and how he could use them to influence people.

Charlie started to attract a group of followers, many of whom were very young women with troubled emotional lives who were rebelling against their parents and society in general. He battered down their inhibitions and questioned the validity of their notions of good and evil. For the most part, Charlie's followers were weak-willed people who were naïve, gullible and easy to lead. LSD and amphetamines were additional tools by which Charlie altered their personalities to his needs.

In spring of 1968, Manson and his followers left San Francisco in an old school bus and traveled around. Eventually, he and a few of his group moved in with Gary Hinman, a music teacher with a house on the Canyon Road. Through Hinman, Charlie met Dennis Wilson of the Beach Boys. Manson and his girls starting hanging around Wilson every chance they had. Manson tried to leverage the acquaintance with Dennis Wilson but it didn't go anywhere. Eventually, Wilson became uncomfortable with Manson and his girls and told them to split.

About that time, Manson found George Spahn and conned the old man into letting him and his followers live on the Ranch. Squeaky Fromme, one of Charlie's devotees, made sure that the elderly man's sexual needs were fully satisfied. The Manson Family survived by a combination of stealing and scavenging. Much of their food was taken from what the supermarkets discard each day.

Charlie was still hell-bent to market his music to somebody. Through his contacts with Dennis Wilson and another man in the music business, Charlie met Doris Day's son Terry Melcher. The plan was to interest Melcher in financing a film with Manson's music.

At that time, Melcher owned the house on Cielo Drive that was eventually leased to Roman Polanski and Sharon Tate. At various times, Manson had been by the property in a car with Dennis Wilson.

Melcher was asked to listen to Charlie and decide whether or not he wanted to record them. Melcher went out the first time and listened to Charlie sing his own compositions and play the guitar. Some of the girls sang and played tambourines. Melcher went out a second time a week later, but the music was nothing he was interested in recording. What he didn't realize is that Manson had built this recording opportunity with Melcher into something very real in his mind. When nothing came of it, Charlie was plenty angry and blamed Melcher for his disappointment.

Helter Skelter

Another facet of Charlie, although not nearly as important to him as his music, was his philosophy. To a large extent, this "philosophy" was a con, something he dreamed up to impress his followers, but he probably believed some of it.

The core of this philosophy was a kind of Armageddon. Charlie preached that the black man was going to rise up and start killing the whites and turn the cities in to an inferno of racial revenge. The black man would win this war, but wouldn't be able to hang onto the power he seized because of innate inferiority.

In 1968, Charlie was forecasting racial war when all of a sudden the Beatles released their White Album, which had the song "Helter Skelter." The lyrics fit Charlie's theory to a tee: "Look out helter skelter helter skelter helter skelter/She's coming down fast/ Yes she is/Yes she is." Now, the racial Armageddon had a name. It was Helter Skelter.

Helter Skelter would begin, according to one of Charlie's devotees, "with the black man going into white people's homes and ripping off the white people, physically destroying them. A couple of spades from Watts would come up into the Bel Air and Beverly Hills district...and just really wipe some people out, just cutting bodies up and smearing blood and writing things on the wall in blood...all kinds of super-atrocious crimes that would really make the white man mad...until there was open revolution in the streets, until they finally won and took over. Then the black man would assume the white man's karma. He would then be the establishment..."

Charlie and the Family would survive this racial holocaust because they would be hiding in the desert safe from the turmoil of the cities. He pulled from the Book of Revelations, the concept of a "bottomless pit," the entrance of which, according to Charlie, was a cave underneath Death Valley that led down to a city of gold. This paradise was where Charlie and his Family were going to wait out this war. Afterwards, when the black man failed at keeping power, Charlie's Family, which they estimated would have multiplied to 144,000 by that time, would then take over from the black man and rule the cities.

"It will be our world then," Charlie told his followers. "There would be no one else, except for us and the black servants. He, Charles Willis Manson, the fifth angel, Jesus Christ, would then rule the world. The other four angels were the Beatles.

How did this hokey philosophy result in the blood bath at the Tate and LaBianca houses? Well, Charlie the Prophet had already forecast that the murders would start in the summer of 1969, but as the summer went on, it looked as though the "prophet" was wrong. "The only thing blackie knows is what whitey has told him," he said to one of his followers just before the murders. "I'm going to have to show him how to do it."

After the LaBianca murder, one of Manson's girls, Linda Kasabian, was told to take Rosemary LaBianca's wallet and credit cards and leave them in the ladies room of a gas station in an area heavily populated by blacks. That way, when, theoretically, the credit cards would be used by some black woman, it would appear that blacks were responsible for the LaBianca deaths. However, the credit cards were never used or turned in to the authorities.

Prosecution

Vincent Bugliosi

On November 18, 1969, 35-year-old Deputy District Attorney Vincent T. Bugliosi was assigned the Tate-LaBianca murder cases. Aaron Stovitz, head of the Trials Division of the District Attorney's Office, was assigned as a co-prosecutor, but was later pulled off for another case.

Bugliosi had an unbelievably difficult job ahead of him. Not only did he need to prove that members of the Manson Family were responsible for the Tate and LaBianca murders, but he had to prove the Charles Manson ordered them to do it. While Manson had sent four Family members to the Cielo Drive massacre, he did not go himself. He did, however, tie up Rosemary and Leno LaBianca and gave three others instructions to kill them.

The prosecutor had to establish Charlie's dominance over the members of his Family and convince a jury that Charlie had sufficient motive to want these seven people dead.

Charles (Tex) Watson

At the beginning, he didn't have much of a case. There was Susan Atkins' story as related to Virginia Graham and the stories that Al Springer and Danny DeCarlo told the police, along with some comments from other people interviewed about Manson and his followers. It wasn't until December 3 that Bugliosi knew for certain who of Manson's Family had actually been involved with the murders. Manson had sent Charles "Tex" Watson, Susan Atkins, Patricia Krenwinkel, and Linda Kasabian to the Tate residence. Accompanying him to the LaBianca home was Watson, Krenwinkel, and Leslie Van Houten. Atkins, Kasabian and Steve "Clem" Grogan waited in the car.

Atkins' testimony was deemed vital to the prosecution, but she was not offered immunity. However, if she cooperated with the prosecution, they would not seek the death penalty against her in any of the three cases: Hinman, Tate and LaBianca. The extent to which she cooperated would affect whether the prosecution would press for first-degree murder, life sentence, etc.

Things started to look up for the prosecution when a fingerprint of Patricia Krenwinkel's was found on a door inside of Sharon Tate's bedroom. This physical evidence was added to the .22 caliber bullets found at the Spahn Ranch (the gun used at the Tate murders was a .22 caliber revolver).

The first order of business for Bugliosi was to get grand jury indictments against Manson and the individuals involved in the murders. When Susan Atkins testified to the grand jury, she gave the same bloodcurdling story to them that she gave to Ronnie Howard and Virginia Graham. She showed absolutely no sign of guilt or remorse for the ghastly things she did. The jurors stared at her in disbelief.

Biker Danny DeCarlo testified that he, Manson, Watson and others had used a .22 caliber Buntline revolver for target practice at the Spahn Ranch.

He also said that the three-strand nylon rope that was used in the Tate murders was identical to the rope used at the ranch.

Linda Kasabian

It only took the grand jury twenty minutes to hand down the indictments Bugliosi sought: Charles Manson, Charles "Tex" Watson, Patricia Krenwinkel, Susan Atkins, and Linda Kasabian, seven counts of murder and one count of conspiracy to commit murder; Leslie van Houten, two counts of murder and one count of conspiracy to commit murder.

Evidence

A few days later, the wallet belonging to Rosemary LaBianca was found in the ladies restroom at the service station where Linda Kasabian left it. The wallet had gotten lodged in the toilet tank. This piece of corroborating evidence was necessary to bolster Susan Atkins' story in case she decided to repudiate her testimony when Charlie started to pressure her.

Another critical piece of evidence was finally "found:" the unusual .22 caliber Hi Standard Longhorn revolver with the broken gun grip which had been found by Bernard Weiss' son and turned over to the police three and a half months earlier. Bernard Weiss after reading about the indictments in the newspaper called LAPD Homicide to see if the revolver he had turned in was the murder weapon.

After being passed around to several people, an officer told Weiss "We don't keep guns that long. We throw them in the ocean after a while."

Weiss said, "I can't believe that you'd throw away what could be the single most important piece of evidence in the Tate case."

Leslie Van Houten

"Listen, mister," was the official answer. "We can't check out every citizen report on every gun we find."

Weiss called a newscaster, who in turn, called the LAPD. The gun was "found" where it had been "lost" in the Van Nuys police station. After the tests had been run, there was no doubt that it was the murder weapon. One thing remained to be done — linking Manson to that particular revolver. Eventually Randy Starr provided that link. He once owned the revolver and had given it to Manson.

Another important development occurred when the police were contacted by the man who owned the place that the Tate killers had used to clean up right after the murders. The man had remembered the car and the license plate, which was traced to a Spahn Ranch employee, who had let Manson and his girls borrow his car.

Motive

Manson mugshot

Even though it was not necessary for the prosecution to establish the motive for the crimes, Bugliosi considered motive an important piece of evidence, especially since Manson was not physically present at the Tate murders. Bugliosi set out to establish that the primary motive was Helter Skelter: Manson's belief that he could start a race war and personally gain from it. But certainly, there was the connection between Manson's anger at Terry Melcher and the crimes committed on his former property. To further bolster that motive, it was established that two different people had chased Manson off the property a few months before the murders.

Rudi Altobelli, the man who bought the Cielo Drive property from Melcher, was an important man in the entertainment industry. He represented stars like Katherine Hepburn and Henry Fonda. Because he traveled so much, he rented out the property to the Polanski's and stayed in the guesthouse when he visited the area.

In March of 1969, Manson went to the house where four of the five murdered people were staying. Charlie said he was looking for Melcher. Sharon's houseguest sent him away in not too friendly terms, but not before he saw Sharon, who wondered what the "creepy looking guy" wanted.

Then Manson went to the guesthouse and told Rudi Altobelli that the people in the main house told him to ask at the guesthouse. Altobelli admonished Manson for bothering his tenants and told him he didn't know where Terry Melcher had moved.

Manson knew the layout of the house and he knew who was living in it. It was quite possible that the "Helter Skelter" crimes were committed at that particular house because Charlie wanted to pay back the residents for rejecting him and scare the daylights out of Melcher for not backing his recording career.

Manson himself became a major player as he appeared frequently in the courtroom. Bugliosi studied him and described the behavior he witnessed:

Though he had little formal schooling, he was fairly articulate, and definitely bright. He picked up little nuances, seemed to consider all of the hidden sides of a question before answering. His moods were mercurial, his facial expressions chameleon-like. Underneath, however, there was a strange intensity. You felt it even when he was joking, which, despite the seriousness of the charges, was often. He frequently played to the always-packed courtroom, not only to the Family faithful but to the press and spectators as well. Spotting a pretty girl, he'd often smile or wink. Usually they appeared more flattered than offended.

The Trial

The trial officially began in mid-June of 1970. Judge Charles Older presided. He decided that the jury, once selected, would be locked up until the end of the trial — "to protect them from harassment and to prevent their being exposed to trial publicity." Older was given a bodyguard and his home was provided with protection.

The twelve jurors selected were five women and seven men with a range of ages spanning from 25 to 73. While many occupations were represented, one was a retired deputy sheriff.

In his opening statement, Bugliosi characterized Manson as "vagrant wanderer, a frustrated singer-guitarist...who would refer to himself as Jesus Christ...and was a killer who cleverly masqueraded behind the common image of a hippie that of being peace loving...but was a megalomaniac who coupled his insatiable thirst for power with an intense obsession for violent death."

Bugliosi stressed that Manson commanded his followers to commit the murders, but that "the evidence will show that they were very willing participants in these mass murders..."

Manson, who first appeared to the jury with a bloody X that he had carved into his forehead, insisted on defending himself. He was assisted by an older lawyer named Irving Kanarek, who was legendary for his attention to detail (much to the frustration of witnesses, judges and juries) and Ronald Hughes, "the hippie lawyer" who was Leslie Van Houten's attorney.

Critical to Manson's defense was maintaining control of the Family. If his followers testified against him, he was doomed. He had to set up and maintain an effective communications network between himself and the other Family members, particularly those under indictment. He needed the Family members who were not in jail to communicate his wishes to those who were.

Just how sinister this communication would be was evidenced by what happened to Barbara Hoyt. Hoyt was one of the prosecution's witnesses, who was threatened that if she testified at the trial, she and her family would be killed. She was then lured to Honolulu by one of Manson's girls and given a lethal dose of LSD. Fortunately, she got to the hospital in time for doctors to save her.

Manson was able to exert a lot of control over his girls in the courtroom. By then Susan Atkins had repudiated her testimony to the grand jury. They came up with bizarre stories that would implicate themselves but spare their beloved Charlie.

As the evidence was presented, things were looking bad for Charlie and the girls. A pattern was developing, according to Bugliosi: "The more damaging the testimony, the more chance that Manson would create a disturbance, thereby assuring that he — and not the evidence itself — would get the day's headlines. Often these disturbances would result in Judge Older removing them from the courtroom.

The drama hit a high point when Manson got into an argument with Judge Older and jumped towards the judge, yelling, "someone should cut your head off!" Atkins, Krenwinkel and Van Houten stood up and started chanting in Latin.

When Manson and his girls were removed from the court, a shaken Judge Older instructed the jury to disregard what they heard and saw, but the effect was indelible. The jury got a first hand chance to see the real Charles Manson.

After 22 weeks of trial, the Prosecution rested. It was time for the defense attorneys to do their part. Judge Older told the lawyers that were assisting Manson and defending the girls to call their first witness. The defense responded: "Thank you, Your Honor. The defendants rest."

The court was stunned. Then the three girls shouted that they wanted to testify. The judge and everyone else was bewildered. The girls had decided that they would testify that *they* planned and committed the murders themselves and that Charlie had nothing to do with it.

Ronald Hughes, Leslie Van Houten's "hippie lawyer" objected and stood up against Manson's transparent ploy: "I refuse to take part in any proceeding where I am forced to push a client out the window." A few days later, Ronald Hughes had disappeared. After the trial was over, his body was found wedged between two boulders in Ventura County. One of Manson's followers later admitted that the Manson Family had murdered him.

A new lawyer had to be found immediately to take over the defense. Maxwell Keith was appointed. When the court reconvened, Manson and the girls created a disturbance suggesting that Judge Older "did away with Ronald Hughes," which resulted in them being removed again from the courtroom.

For the most part, the lawyers for the defense put forth a disappointing presentation. Paul Fitzgerald, Patricia Krenwinkel's attorney, spent more time defending Manson than his client. Daye Shinn, Susan Atkins' lawyer made a brief defense for his client. Irving Kanarek went on for days in his rambling style. Finally, Judge Older accused him of filibustering. Manson, apparently also tired of Kanarek's exhausting argument, shouted at him: "Why don't you sit down? You're just making things worse."

Verdict

Vanhouten, Atkin and Krenwinkel return to court

On January 15, 1971, seven months after the start of the trial, the jury began to deliberate. Nine days later, it came to a verdict. Security was very tight around the Hall of Justice since a Manson follower had stolen a case of hand grenades from a Marine Base and reportedly had planned a special event on what they were calling "Judgment Day."

The jury had found Charles Manson, Patricia Krenwinkel, Susan Atkins and Leslie Van Houten each guilty of murder and conspiracy to commit murder.

Charles "Tex" Watson, because of extradition proceedings and other legal complications did not stand trial until later in the year and was also found guilty of murder and conspiracy to commit murder.

Manson Girls shave their heads after Manson verdict

On March 29, 1971, the jury completed deliberations on the penalty phase of the trial. Manson and the three female defendants had shaved their heads for the reading of their verdicts.

"We, the jury in the above-entitled action, having found the defendant Charles Manson guilty of murder in the first degree...do now fix the penalty as death."

Patricia Krenwinkel responded: "You have just judged yourselves."

"Better lock your doors and watch your own kids," Susan Atkins said.

All four defendants received the death penalty.

On April 19, 1971, Superior Court Judge Charles H. Older pronounced the judgment: "It is my considered judgment that not only is the death penalty appropriate, but it is almost compelled by the circumstances. I must agree with the prosecutor that if this is not a proper case for the death penalty, what should be?"

The judge shook the hands of each juror. "If it were within the power of a trial judge to award a medal of honor to jurors, believe me, I would bestow an award on each of you."

At a later date, Robert Beausoleil, Charles Manson, Charles Watson, Bruce Davis and Steve Grogan were tried and convicted for the murders of Gary Hinman and Donald (Shorty) Shea.

Bugliosi wrote," it had been the longest murder trial in American history, lasting nine and a half months; the most expensive, costing approximately $1 million; and the most highly publicized; while the jury had been sequestered 225 days, longer than any jury before it. The trial transcript alone ran to 209 volumes, 31,716 pages, approximately eight million words."

In 1972, the California Supreme Court abolished the death penalty in the state and all of the defendants are serving life sentences.

Afterward

Right after the trial, there were a number of articles written that were favorable to Manson and his followers. For a while, it appeared that he might become some sort of cult hero. That never really materialized, however, and there is very little left of the Manson Family today. However, Manson still receives a large amount of mail, much of it from young people who want to join the Family.

Lynette Fromme

There have been several plays about him, movies and documentaries and even an opera. Charlie's music has been played by the Guns N' Roses rock band.

Why, when other murderers that were responsible for many more deaths than Manson are forgotten by most people, does Manson remain so notorious?

Perhaps because the people they murdered and the ones they planned to murder were celebrities. Also, perhaps because of Lynette "Squeaky" Fromme's failed attempt to assassinate President Gerald Ford in 1975, even though it is unlikely that Manson put her up to it.

Bugliosi believes the notoriety continues because it is the most bizarre and strange, almost unbelievable, murder case in history. He thinks that Manson has become a "metaphor" for evil, catapulting him to near mythological proportions...People worry about this man the way they worry about cancer and earthquakes."

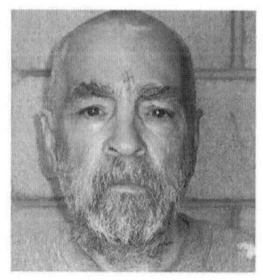

An older Manson

Manson endures, even as a sixty-year old, comparatively passive prisoner, unlikely to ever be paroled. Bugliosi sums up the continued fascination with the more fanatical elements of society: "Today, almost every disaffected and morally twisted group in America, from Satanists to neo-Nazi skinheads, has embraced Manson and the poisons of his virulent philosophy. He has become their spiritual icon, the high priest of anti-establishment hatred."

Where Are They Now?

Charles Manson

Charles Manson Then

Charles Manson Now

In 1989, Nikolas Schreck conducted an interview of
Manson, cutting the interview up for material in his
documentary *Charles Manson Superstar*. This was the first,
and is considered one of the most authoritative and
comprehensive, documentaries on the subject. Schreck
concluded that the story behind the murders was probably
false, and that an admitted plan, by several of the women at
the ranch interviewed after the trial was concluded,
involved killing the people at the Tate home in order to free
Bobby Beausoleil as per an attempt to copycat the murder
of Gary Hinman. According to this, the use of writings of
blood on the walls at the Tate and LaBianca residences was
merely a ploy to make it seem that the murderer of Hinman

was still free, and that Beausoleil was not guilty. Key in his refutation of the hypothesis was the fact that, while the prosecution attempted to show Manson ordered the killings because he was upset over Terry Melcher (and believed Melcher to still be at that address), this could certainly not have been the case, as Manson attempted on several occasions to contact Melcher at his new address, showing he knew very well Melcher no longer lived at the Tate home. Schreck also concluded that Manson was not insane, but merely acting that way out of frustration.

On September 25, 1984, while imprisoned at the California Medical Facility at Vacaville, Manson was severely burned by a fellow inmate who poured paint thinner on him and set him alight. The other prisoner, Jan Holmstrom, explained that Manson had objected to his Hare Krishna chants and had verbally threatened him. Despite suffering second- and third-degree burns over 20 percent of his body, Manson recovered from his injuries. In December 1987, Fromme, serving a life sentence for the assassination attempt, escaped briefly from Alderson Federal Prison Camp in West Virginia. She was trying to reach Manson, who she had heard had testicular cancer; she was apprehended within days. She was released on parole from Federal Medical Center, Carswell on August 14, 2009.

Later events

In a 1994 conversation with Manson prosecutor Vincent Bugliosi, Catherine Share, a one-time Manson-follower, stated that her testimony in the penalty phase of Manson's trial had been a fabrication intended to save Manson from the gas chamber and had been given on Manson's explicit direction. Share's testimony had introduced the copycat-motive story, which the testimony of the three female defendants echoed and according to which the Tate-LaBianca murders had been Linda Kasabian's idea. In a 1997 segment of the tabloid television program *Hard Copy*, Share implied that her testimony had been given under a Manson threat of physical harm. In August 1971, after Manson's trial and sentencing, Share had participated in a violent California retail store robbery, the object of which was the acquisition of weapons to help free Manson.

In January 1996, a Manson website was established by latter-day Manson follower George Stimson, who was helped by Sandra Good. Good had been released from prison in 1985, after serving 10 years of her 15-year sentence for the death threats. The Manson website, ATWA.com, was discontinued in 2001, but as of 2011, it was running again, but currently the domain is up for sale and the website is discontinued.

In June 1997, Manson was found to have been trafficking in drugs by a prison disciplinary committee. That August, he was moved from Corcoran State Prison to Pelican Bay State Prison.

In a 1998–99 interview in *Seconds* magazine, Bobby Beausoleil rejected the view that Manson ordered him to kill Gary Hinman. He stated Manson did come to Hinman's house and slash Hinman with a sword. In a 1981 interview with *Oui* magazine, he denied this. Beausoleil stated that when he read about the Tate murders in the newspaper, "I wasn't even sure at that point – really, I had no idea who had done it until Manson's group were actually arrested for it. It had only crossed my mind and I had a premonition, perhaps. There was some little tickle in my mind that the killings might be connected with them ..." In the *Oui* magazine interview, he had stated, "When the Tate-LaBianca murders happened, I knew who had done it. I was fairly certain."

William Garretson, once the young caretaker at Cielo Drive, indicated in a program broadcast in July 1999 on *E!*, that he had, in fact, seen and heard a portion of the Tate murders from his location in the property's guest house. This comported with the unofficial results of the polygraph examination that had been given to Garretson on August 10, 1969, and that had effectively eliminated him as a suspect. The LAPD officer who conducted the examination had concluded Garretson was "clean" on participation in the crimes but "muddy" as to his having heard anything. Garretson did not explain why he had withheld his knowledge of the events.

Later developments

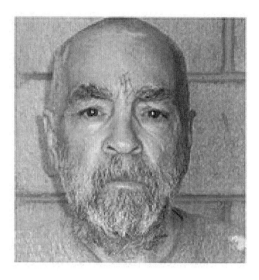

Manson at age 74 (March 2009)

On September 5, 2007, MSNBC aired *The Mind of Manson*, a complete version of a 1987 interview at California's San Quentin State Prison. The footage of the "unshackled, unapologetic, and unruly" Manson had been considered "so unbelievable" that only seven minutes of it had originally been broadcast on *The Today Show*, for which it had been recorded.

In a January 2008 segment of the Discovery Channel's *Most Evil*, Barbara Hoyt said that the impression that she had accompanied Ruth Ann Moorehouse to Hawaii just to avoid testifying at Manson's trial was erroneous. Hoyt said she had cooperated with the Family because she was "trying to keep them from killing my family." She stated that, at the time of the trial, she was "constantly being threatened: 'Your family's gonna die. The murders could be repeated at your house.'"

On March 15, 2008, the Associated Press reported that forensic investigators had conducted a search for human remains at Barker Ranch the previous month. Following up on longstanding rumors that the Family had killed hitchhikers and runaways who had come into its orbit during its time at Barker, the investigators identified "two likely clandestine grave sites ... and one additional site that merits further investigation." Though they recommended digging, CNN reported on March 28 that the Inyo County sheriff, who questioned the methods they employed with search dogs, had ordered additional tests before any excavation. On May 9, after a delay caused by damage to test equipment, the sheriff announced that test results had been inconclusive and that "exploratory excavation" would begin on May 20. In the meantime, Tex Watson had commented publicly that "no one was killed" at the desert camp during the month-and-a-half he was there, after the Tate-LaBianca murders. On May 21, after two days of work, the sheriff brought the search to an end; four potential gravesites had been dug up and had been found to hold no human remains. In March 2009, a photograph taken of a 74-year old Manson, showing a receding hairline, grizzled gray beard and hair and the swastika tattoo still prominent on his forehead, was released to the public by California corrections officials.

In September 2009, The History Channel broadcast a docudrama covering the Family's activities and the murders as part of its coverage on the 40th anniversary of the killings. The program included an in-depth interview with Linda Kasabian, who spoke publicly for the first time since a 1989 appearance on *A Current Affair*, an American television news magazine. Also included in the History

Channel program were interviews with Vincent Bugliosi, Catherine Share, and Debra Tate, sister of Sharon.

As the 40th anniversary of the Tate-LaBianca murders approached, in July 2009, *Los Angeles* magazine published an "oral history", in which former Family members, law-enforcement officers, and others involved with Manson, the arrests, and the trials offered their recollections of—and observations on—the events that made Manson notorious. In the article, Juan Flynn, a Spahn Ranch worker who had become associated with Manson and the Family, said, "Charles Manson got away with everything. People will say, 'He's in jail.' But Charlie is exactly where he wants to be."

In November 2009, a Los Angeles DJ and songwriter named Matthew Roberts released correspondence and other evidence indicating he had been biologically fathered by Manson. Roberts' biological mother claims to have been a member of the Manson Family who left in the summer of 1967 after being raped by Manson; the mother returned to her parents' home to complete the pregnancy, gave birth on March 22, 1968, and subsequently gave up Roberts for adoption. Manson himself has stated that he "could" be the father, acknowledging the biological mother and a sexual relationship with her during 1967; this was nearly two years before the Family began its murderous phase.

In 2010, the *Los Angeles Times* reported that Manson was caught with a cell phone in 2009, and had contacted people in California, New Jersey, Florida and British Columbia. A spokesperson for the California Department of Corrections stated that it was not known if Manson had used the phone for criminal purposes.

On October 4, 2012, Bruce Davis, who had been convicted of the murder of Shorty Shea and the attempted robbery by Manson Family members of a Hawthorne gun shop in 1971, was recommended for parole by the California Department of Corrections at his 27th parole hearing. In 2010, Governor Arnold Schwarzenegger had reversed the board's previous finding in favor of Davis, denying him parole for two more years. On March 1, 2013, Governor Jerry Brown also denied parole for Davis.

Parole hearings

Manson at age 76 in June 2011

A footnote to the conclusion of *California v. Anderson*, the 1972 decision that neutralized California's then-current death sentences, stated, "Any prisoner now under a sentence of death ... may file a petition for writ of habeas corpus in the superior court inviting that court to modify its judgment to provide for the appropriate alternative punishment of life imprisonment or life imprisonment without possibility of parole specified by statute for the crime for which he was sentenced to death." This made Manson eligible to apply for parole after seven years' incarceration. His first parole hearing took place on

November 16, 1978, at the California Medical Facility in Vacaville.

Manson was denied parole for the 12th time on April 11, 2012. Manson did not attend the hearing where prison officials argued that Manson had a history of controlling behavior and mental health issues including schizophrenia and paranoid delusional disorder and was too great a danger to be released. It was determined that Manson would not be reconsidered for parole for another 15 years, at which time he would be 92 years old.

His California Department of Corrections and Rehabilitation inmate number at Corcoran State Prison is B33920.

Charles Manson, 79, to marry girlfriend 'Star,' 25?

She says yes; he says 'garbage'

Murderer Manson is still doing life in Corcoran Prison for the Tate-LaBianca slayings — His girlfriend wants the world to know that he is her 'husband.'

Charles Manson is to marry his 25-year-old girlfriend behind bars, she has claimed.

In an interview with Rolling Stone magazine, the young woman who calls herself "Star," tells the world that she is to be the next bride of the 79-year-old.

"I'll tell you straight up, Charlie and I are going to get married," she told Rolling Stone magazine. "When that will be, we don't know. But I take it very seriously. Charlie is my husband. Charlie told me to tell you this. We haven't told anybody about that.

"People can think I'm crazy. But they don't know. This is what's right for me. This is what I was born for," she told the magazine. The pair has been in a relationship since "Star" was 19.

She began visiting him at Corcoran State Prison in
California when she was still a teenager. She is originally
from Missouri.

"Star" has even cut an "X" into her forehead, in an apparent
twisted homage to Mason's swastika symbol.

Manson has been incarcerated for 44 years since the cult
leader was convicted of the murders of actress Sharon Tate
and Leno and Rosemary LaBianco.

Manson, who has been married twice before, denied the
claim of marriage.

"That's a bunch of garbage. You know that, man. That's
trash. We're just playing that for public consumption," he
told Rolling Stone. He also revealed that he was bisexual.

Manson said: "Sex to me is like going to the toilet. Whether
it's a girl or not, it doesn't matter."

Star began visiting Manson at Corcoran State Prison in California when she was still a teenager.

Charles Manson with Star, who says they are to marry. But Manson says, "That's a bunch of garbage. You know that, man. That's trash. We're just playing that for public consumption."

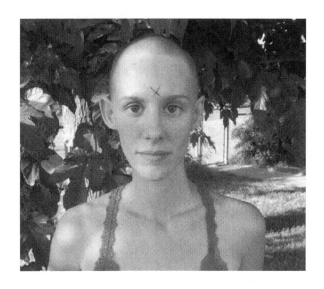

Star said in Rolling Stone magazine, "I'll tell you straight up, Charlie and I are going to get married."

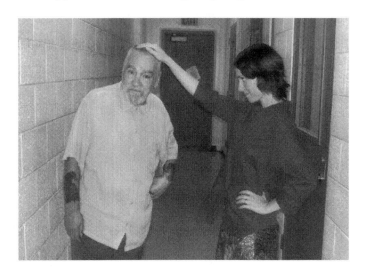

Star says of her relationship with Manson, "this is what's right for me. This is what I was born for."

Forensic Science

and

The Charles

Manson Murders

Advancements in Forensic Technologies

The capture and conviction of Charles Manson took over
one and a half years to complete. Within this time period
many law enforcement officers and forensics professionals
put in countless numbers of hours collecting, preserving
and testing the physical evidence they found. In addition,
the forensics practices used in this case as well as the police
investigation techniques serve as a valuable lesson for those
in these fields today. In this paper we will look at some of
the crimes that were committed by the Manson Family, the
mishandled investigation that followed and the forensic
techniques used to aid (and sometimes hinder the efforts) in
obtaining convictions against those involved.

The first five murders, later to be called the "Tate" murders,
occurred in a house high above the city of Los Angeles.
One victim (Steven Parent) was found in his car outside the
house and he had been shot four times and stabbed once.

Another two victims (Abigail Folger and Voytek Frykowski) were found on the back lawn of the Tate estate. Coroner's reports would later indicate that Abigail had been stabbed twenty-eight times and Voytek was shot twice, struck over the head thirteen times and stabbed Sebring were found inside the house tied together by a rope around their necks, which was hung over a rafter in the ceiling. Sharon, who was eight months pregnant at the time, had died from multiple stab wounds to the chest and back, totaling sixteen. Jay, who was found with Sharon, had been stabbed seven times and shot once. He died of exsanguination, which is bleeding to death and neither of the victims had actually died from hanging. The next two victims, in what would become known as the "LaBianca" murders, were found in a home in the Los Feliz section of Los Angeles. Leno and Rosemary LaBianca were found stabbed to death in their home. He had been stabbed multiple times and a knife and fork were found protruding from his body and she had been stabbed forty-one times. The departments working on the two investigations were the Los Angeles Sheriff's Office (LASO) (LaBianca) and the Los Angeles Police Department (LAPD) (Tate). This would later play a very important role in the investigation in the year and a half due to mass miscommunication between the two departments concerning the two crime scenes.

Lack of communication between the two law enforcement entities put both cases in jeopardy several times during the investigations. For example, the word "PIG" was printed on the door at the Tate scene and the detectives from the LASO approached LAPD detectives and told them of the writing of the words "Death to Pigs" in the victim 'sown blood at the LaBianca scene. When presented with possible evidence that the two crimes might be linked, Los Angeles Police Department (LAPD) inspector K.J. McCauley told reporters "I don't see any connection between this murder (Tate) and the others. They're too widely removed. I just don't see any connection". This was the official stance taken by the LAPD and the detectives proceeded to work solely on their own cases. In addition to the communication problems, the officers also encountered emotional, political, and mental stress from the shear senselessness of the crimes. One of Manson's most faithful followers would later say "We wanted to do a crime that the world would have to stand up and take notice". As the first officers observed the horrific scene gradually unfold, they began to lose focus of their procedural duties and there were also several mistakes made in the preservation and collection of evidence.

After arriving and securing the scenes officers, proceeded to assess the extent of the damage. What they found was shocking. A macabre scene of a massacre like no one had ever seen before. Upon making the grizzly discoveries the officers became less strict on their adherence to procedure and more intent on finding the killer or killers. The officers got sheets from the linen closet and covered the bodies. One week later the blue sheet that was used to cover Abigail Folger on the lawn would still be there.

Although placing the sheets on the bodies was not a good idea, not transferring them to the lab with the bodies was worse. Police officers, being the first to arrive at the scene of a crime, must follow strict procedures in an effort to protect any shred of evidence that may be needed to obtain a conviction.

LAPD officers made several mistakes that could have potentially seriously damaged the prosecution's case. For example, Officer DeRosa, while he was escorting a possible suspect, down the driveway of the Tate estate noticed that there was blood on the button that opened the electric gate. According to Bugliosi in his book "Helter Skelter",

"Officer DeRosa, who was charged with securing and protecting the scene until investigating officers arrived, now pressed the button himself, successfully opening the gate but also creating a superimpose that obliterated any print that may have been there".

Fingerprints would be a problem area for police throughout the investigations. The gun used in the murders was discovered by a boy in Los Angles about two weeks after the murders. "The boy was careful not to touch the revolver to protect fingerprints. The police smudged it up and filed it away, the chambers of the weapon containing seven spent shells and two live bullets". Although the fingerprints on the gun were obliterated by police officials, forensics professionals were able to match a print from the front door of the Tate residence and one lifted from the frame on the inside door of Sharon Tate's bedroom to two of the suspects. These prints would become an important key to the prosecution's case.

In addition to eradicating fingerprints, officers made several other procedural mistakes. For example, pieces of a gun grip that were first seen near the entryway ended up under a chair in the living room. According to the official LAPD report: "They were apparently kicked under the chair by one of the original officers on the scene...." On December 16 these pieces would be matched to the gun that had been in police custody since September 10, 1969 when the Los Angles boy had found it in his yard. Police probably would never have made the connection if the boy's father, having heard about the caliber of gun used in the murders, had not insisted that the police check it out. Since guns and other property are routinely disposed of after a period of time, prosecutors were rather lucky that the gun was still around.

Officers were also unable to locate any of the knives or bloody clothing from the murders. One of the Manson accomplices (Susan Atkins) divulged to a cell mate her involvement in the crimes, including a suggestion of the location where these items were thrown from the vehicle. A television news crew set out to find them. They used statements made by Atkins, such as "mountain on one side" and "ravine on the other" to guide their search. On December 15, much to the chagrin of the police, they found the clothing.

Forensic professionals were also lacking in the performance of their duties. One in particular, Officer Joe Granado, a forensic chemist assigned to both cases, failed to note or sample blood spatters around the bushes where someone had apparently fallen at the Tate residence. He also did not take samples from the pools of blood around the two bodies in the living room, nor from the two bodies on the lawn. He later testified that he presumed that the blood surrounding the victims was their own and he would get those samples from the coroner later. Granado obtained forty-five blood samples from the Tate scene and he failed to run subtypes on twenty-one of those. Two days later at the LaBianca scene he would take no subtypes which would cause major complications later in the trial. On the walkway leading to the Tate residence were several large pools of blood and Granado only took a sample from one of these pools, "presuming, he later said, all were the same". Unfortunately, officers at the scene tracked blood from inside the residence onto the front porch and walkway and back again, which compounded the problems. This made it necessary to interview all the individuals' who had been at the scene about the shoes they had worn that day.

Although all these mistakes were made, officials were still able to put together enough evidence for trial. During the trial obvious signs of Manson's control over the family members was exhibited. At one point, Manson turned around and refused to face the judge. His followers, as well as his co-defendants did the same. When he shaved his head or carved an X in his forehead, they did too. He would also make periodic outbursts from time to time in the courtroom which his followers would repeat in a chant-like manner. All of these theatrics worked to the detriment of the defendants. Manson and four of his followers were subsequently convicted on all counts. This is somewhat extraordinary, because Manson never actually was present at the Tate murder scene.

"Prosecutor Vincent Bugliosi was faced with a difficult endeavor as it was. He proved that Manson, although not a direct participant, had ordered the Tate-LaBianca killings". He was present at the LaBianca scene, only long enough to tie up the victims. He then walked outside and told his followers to "kill them." All of the defendants were sentenced to death which was later commuted to life when California's laws were changed. Although he has come up for parole several times already there is little doubt as to whether he will remain in prison.

At various times Charles Manson's "family" numbered a hundred or more. Most of those have faded away. However, if you look around you can still find stragglers. The technological age has given birth to a new type of Manson follower, those with their own home pages on the internet. While researching this subject I came across at least 100 pages of information from the faithful. The consolation to this scary strategy is that forensics practices have advanced technologically, also. Errors committed by the officials in the Manson investigation are less often repeated in light of the advanced collection and procedural techniques of today. The murders committed at the command of this lone madman were astounding and senseless. Fortunately the investigation, although mishandled, produced convictions for all involved.

Leslie Van Houten

Leslie Van Houten Then

Leslie Van Houten Now

Former Charles Manson follower Leslie Van Houten was denied parole June 5, 2013 for the 20th time.

Van Houten, 63, told a California parole board in unprecedented detail how committed she was to the murders Manson ordered and asserted she has changed and is trying to live a life of healing.

But Board of Parole Hearings Commissioner Jeffrey Ferguson told Van Houten she had failed to explain how someone as intelligent and well-bred as she was could have committed the "cruel and atrocious" murders of Leno and Rosemary La Bianca, and the panel rejected her bid.

Van Houten will be eligible for another parole hearing in five years.

"I know I did something that is unforgiveable, but I can create a world where I make amends," Van Houten said. "I'm trying to be someone who lives a life for healing rather than destruction."

The panel was also heard from relatives of the victims who were starkly opposed to her parole.

"There are certain crimes that are so heinous, so atrocious, so horrible that it should cause denial of parole."

— L.A. County Deputy District Attorney Patrick Sequiera

Van Houten was convicted of murder and conspiracy for her role in the slayings of wealthy Los Angeles grocers Leno and Rosemary La Bianca. They were stabbed to death in August 1969, one night after Manson's followers killed actress Sharon Tate and four others.

Van Houten did not participate in the Tate killings but went along the next night when the La Bianca's were slain in their home. During the penalty phase of her trial she confessed to joining in stabbing Mrs. La Bianca after she was dead.

With survivors of the LaBiancas sitting behind her at the California Institution for Women, Van Houten acknowledged participating in the killings ordered by Manson.

"He could never have done what he did without people like me," said Van Houten, who has been in custody for 44 years.

After years of therapy and self-examination, she said, she realizes that what she did was "like a pebble falling in a pond which affected so many people."

"I know I did something that is unforgiveable, but I can create a world where I make amends."

— Leslie Van Houten

"Mr. and Mrs. La Bianca died the worst possible deaths a human being can," she said.

Arguing to the board, Los Angeles County Deputy District Attorney Patrick Sequiera said some crimes may be an exception to the law guaranteeing the possibility of parole.

"There are certain crimes that are so heinous, so atrocious, so horrible that it should cause denial of parole," he said, elaborating on Van Houten's contradictions over the years.

In response, Van Houten's lawyer, Michael Satris, said his client "sank to the depths of Dante's inferno and she put herself there by consorting with the devil himself, Charles Manson."

Leslie Van Houten appears during her parole hearing with her attorney, Michael Satris, left, on at the California Institution for Women in Chino, Calif.

However, Satris said his client has totally reformed herself.

"Leslie committed a great sin, a great crime in 1969, and in that time (in prison) she has developed into the equal of a saint," he said. "Everything she does is for humanity."

Van Houten was portrayed at trial by her defense lawyers as the youngest and least culpable of those convicted with Manson, a young woman from a good family who had been a homecoming princess and showed promise until she became involved with drugs and was recruited into Manson's murderous cult.

Now deeply wrinkled with long gray hair tied back in a ponytail, Van Houten at times seemed near tears but did not break down at the Wednesday hearing.

She said that when she heard the Manson family had killed Tate and others, she felt left out and asked to go along the second night.

Asked if she would have done the same had children been involved, she answered, "I can't say I wouldn't have done that. I'd like to say I wouldn't, but I don't know."

Asked to explain her actions, she said, "I feel that at that point I had really lost my humanity and I can't know how far I would have gone. I had no regard for life and no measurement of my limitations."

Van Houten has previously been commended for her work helping elderly women inmates at the California Institution for Women. She earned two college degrees while in custody.

Lynette 'Squeaky' Fromme

Lynette 'Squeaky' Fromme Then

Lynette 'Squeaky' Fromme Now

For years she remained one of Manson's loyal followers, corresponding with him after many of his former followers shunned him. A spokeswoman for the prison would not say if they are still in touch.

Murder in Stockton, California

To follow through with Manson's deal with the Aryan Brotherhood, Fromme moved to Stockton, California, with Family member Nancy Pitman and a friend named Priscilla Cooper, and a pair of ex-convict Aryan Brotherhood members named Michael Monfort and James Craig. This group happened to meet up with a couple, James and Lauren Willett, at a cabin. The ex-convicts forced James Willett to dig his own grave and gunned him down because he was going to tell the authorities about a series of robberies that the ex-convicts had committed after they were released from prison. After the body of James Willett was found, with his hand still sticking out of the ground, the housemates were taken into custody on suspicion of murder. After their arrest, the body of Lauren Willett was discovered as well. An infant girl believed to be the Willetts' daughter was also found in the house in Stockton, and placed with Mary Graham Hall. Fromme was released for lack of evidence.

The Sonoma County coroner's office concluded that James Willett was killed sometime in September 1972 although his body was not found until the beginning of November 1972. He had been buried near Guerneville in Sonoma County. On the night of Saturday November 11, 1972, the Stockton Police responded to information that a station wagon owned by the Willetts was in the area. It was discovered parked in front of 720 W. Flora Street. "Police Sgt. Richard Whiteman went to the house and, when he was refused entry, forced his way in. All the persons subsequently arrested were in the house except for Miss Fromme. She telephoned the house while police were there, asking to be picked up, and officers obliged, taking her into custody nearby. Police found a quantity of guns and ammunition in the house along with amounts of marijuana, and noticed freshly dug earth beneath the building."

The Stockton Police obtained a warrant and dug up the body of Lauren Willett around 5 a.m. the following day. Cooper told investigators that Lauren had been shot accidentally and had been buried when they realized she was dead. Cooper contended that Monfort was "demonstrating the dangers of firearms, playing a form of Russian roulette with a .38 caliber pistol" and had first spun the gun cylinder and shot at his own head, and when the gun didn't fire, pointed it at the victim, whereupon it fired. The Stockton Police indicated that Lauren Willett "was with the others of her own volition prior to the shooting, and was not being held prisoner."

Fromme was held in custody for two and a half months but never charged. The other four people involved were convicted. In an interview from the San Joaquin County Jail, she told reporters that she had been traveling in California trying to visit "brothers" in jail and to visit Manson. Fromme said that she came to Stockton to visit William Goucher, who was already in jail on a robbery charge when Mrs. Willett died. She claimed to be innocent of any wrongdoing. "They told me I was being put in here for murder because I didn't have anything to say." She also said from jail, "I know there are lots of people who've spent time for being quiet. That's why Charlie is in jail."

Fromme stated that she took a bus from Los Angeles to Stockton on Friday November 10, 1972, to visit Goucher, whom she described as "a brother". She called Pitman, she said, and spent Friday night at the Flora Street house. When she left the jail after visiting Goucher Saturday, she called the house "to ask someone to pick me up". Stockton Police traced the call and arrested her at a phone booth.

After leaving Stockton, Fromme moved into a Sacramento apartment with fellow Manson family member Sandra Good. The two wore robes on occasion and changed their names to symbolize their devotion to Manson's new religion, Fromme becoming "Red" in honor of her red hair and the redwoods, and Good, "Blue", for her blue eyes and the ocean; both nicknames were originally given to them by Manson.

Attempt to contact

Jimmy Page

In March 1975, during Led Zeppelin's 1975 North American concert tour, Fromme spoke with Danny Goldberg, the vice president of the band's record company at the hotel the band was staying at in L.A. She asked to meet with guitarist Jimmy Page to warn him of "bad energy." Fromme claimed to have foreseen the future and wished to forewarn Page of the imminent danger. Goldberg stated that even he couldn't see Page until the following night, to which Fromme responded "tomorrow night will probably be too late." After a long discussion, Goldberg agreed to deliver a message to Page if she were to commit it to writing. Allegedly, the note was burned.

Assassination attempt on President Ford

On the morning of September 5, 1975, Fromme went to Sacramento's Capitol Park (reportedly to plead with President Gerald Ford about the plight of the California redwoods) dressed in a nun-like red robe and armed with a Colt M1911 .45 semi-automatic pistol that she pointed at Ford. The pistol's magazine was loaded with four rounds, but there was no cartridge in the chamber. She was immediately restrained by Larry Buendorf, a Secret Service agent. While being further restrained and handcuffed, Fromme managed to say a few sentences to the on-scene cameras, emphasizing that the gun "didn't go off". Her 1975 arrest as shown by her sitting in a U.S. Marshal's vehicle as she waits to be brought to jail in 1975 is an image that continues to get frequent use. In 1980, Fromme told *The Sacramento Bee* that she had deliberately ejected the cartridge in her weapon's chamber before leaving home that morning.

After a lengthy trial in which she refused to cooperate with her own defense, she was convicted of the attempted assassination of the president and received a life sentence under a 1965 law which made attempted presidential assassinations a federal crime punishable by a maximum sentence of life in prison. When U.S. Attorney Dwayne Keyes recommended severe punishment because she was "full of hate and violence," Fromme threw an apple at him, hitting him in the face and knocking off his glasses.

"I stood up and waved a gun (at Ford) for a reason," said Fromme. "I was so relieved not to have to shoot it, but, in truth, I came to get life. Not just my life but clean air, healthy water and respect for creatures and creation."

Aftermath

Seventeen days after Fromme's arrest, Sara Jane Moore attempted to assassinate Ford outside the St. Francis Hotel in San Francisco. Moore was restrained by bystander Oliver Sipple, a decorated veteran, and the single shot fired from her gun slightly injured taxi driver John Ludwig, who was standing inside the hotel.

In 1979, Fromme was transferred out of Federal Correctional Institution, Dublin in Dublin, California, for attacking a fellow inmate, Julienne Bušić, with the claw-end of a hammer. On December 23, 1987, she escaped from the Federal Prison Camp, Alderson in Alderson, West Virginia, attempting to meet Manson, who she had heard had testicular cancer. She was captured again two days later and incarcerated at the Federal Medical Center, Carswell in Fort Worth, Texas.

The Colt M1911 .45-caliber pistol used by Fromme in her assassination attempt on Gerald Ford

Fromme first became eligible for parole in 1985, and was entitled by federal law to a mandatory hearing after 30 years, but could waive that hearing and apply for release at a later date. Fromme steadfastly waived her right to request a hearing and was required by federal law to complete a parole application before one could be considered and granted. Fromme was granted parole in July 2008, but was not released because of the extra time added to her sentence for the 1987 prison escape.

Fromme, Federal Bureau of Prisons #06075-180 was released on parole from Federal Medical Center, Carswell on August 14, 2009. She then reportedly moved to Marcy, New York.

Charles "Tex" Watson

Charles "Tex" Watson Then

Charles "Tex" Watson Now

Charles "Tex" Watson is also serving a life sentence for the Tate/LaBianca murders, and is currently housed in Mule Creek State Prison in Northern California.

During his time in prison, Watson has converted to Christianity, written several books, married, fathered four children and trained as a minister of religion. His wife, Kristin and their family live close to the prison where she operates a Web site for their ministry called *Abounding Love Ministries, Inc.*

On October 10, 2001, Watson was turned down again for parole at his thirteenth parole hearing and was told not to apply for another four years.

The Associated Press stated, "Watson made a personal appeal to the two-member panel of the California Board of Prison Terms, saying he takes full responsibility for his crimes and is now a different person who would never do such things again." However, a prison correctional counselor said that "Watson still poses an unpredictable threat to the community should he be released."

Debra Tate, the sister of the brutally murdered Sharon Tate Polanski, tearfully urged the board to deny Watson's request.

His last hearing was in November 2011. He received a five-year denial, rather than a 7-10-15 year maximum.

His next scheduled parole hearing is in November 2016.

Susan "Sadie" Denise Atkins

Susan "Sadie" Denise Atkins Then

Susan "Sadie" Denise Atkins Prison photo

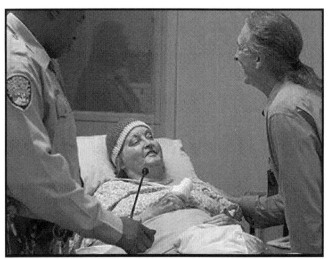

In her last days

Susan "Sadie" Denise Atkins served her life sentence at California Institution for Women at Frontera. During her time in prison Atkins married twice.

In September 2009, at age 61, suffering from terminal brain cancer, Susan Adkins faced her 13th parole hearing. According to a website maintained by her husband and attorney James Whitehouse, with 85 percent of her body paralyzed she could no longer sit up or be moved to a wheelchair. Even so, Whitehouse knew there was still a chance that the parole board would find her release to be a danger to society. Adkins was known among members of the Manson Family as Sadie Mae Glutz, and by her own admission held pregnant actress Sharon Tate down and killed her, stabbing her 16 times. At a parole hearing in 1993 she said that Tate had "asked me to let her baby live....I told her I didn't have any mercy on her."

Vincent Bugliosi, who prosecuted Atkins, said he was not opposed to her release given her current condition, adding that she had paid "substantially, though not completely, for her horrendous crimes. Paying completely would mean imposing the death penalty." Bugliosi also stated that he supported her release in order to save the state money. The cost for Atkins' medical care since she was hospitalized on March 18, 2008, "has reportedly surpassed $1.15 million with additional cost of over $300,000 to guard her hospital room." Bugliosi stated that he was challenging the notion that "just because Susan Atkins showed no mercy to her victims, we therefore are duty-bound to follow her inhumanity and show no mercy to her." Former prosecutor Stephen R. Kay, who also prosecuted Manson supporters, opposed Atkins' release, stating:

Kay also stated that he had attended about 60 parole hearings related to the murders and spent considerable time with the victims' families, witnessing their suffering.

Los Angeles County District Attorney Steve Cooley stated that he was strongly opposed to the release, saying in a letter to the board it would be "an affront to people of this state, the California criminal justice system and the next of kin of many murder victims."

Cooley wrote that Atkins' "horrific crimes alone warrant a denial of her request" and that she "failed to demonstrate genuine remorse and lacks insight and understanding of the gravity of her crimes." Suzan Hubbard, director of adult prisons in California, also recommended against granting Atkins' request. California Governor Arnold Schwarzenegger also opposed Atkins' release, stating that: "I don't believe in compassionate release. I think that they have to stay in, they have to serve their time ... Those kinds of crimes are just so unbelievable that I'm not for the compassionate release."

Orange County District Attorney Tony Rackauckas also opposed Atkins' release, stating that "It would be a grave miscarriage of justice to burden the citizens of Orange County by paroling her to Orange County, where she can enjoy the comforts of her husband, home and mercy she did not show Sharon Tate [or] her unborn baby."

Atkins' release hearing took place on July 15, 2008. During the 90-minute hearing, emotional pleas were made by both supporters and opponents of Atkins' release. The public hearing limited speakers' comments to five minutes each. After the board heard the case (as well as other agenda items), it retired to closed session for final deliberations.

Due to her failing health, Atkins herself did not attend the hearing.

Debra Tate, the only surviving immediate relative of murder victim Sharon Tate, spoke in opposition to a compassionate release for Atkins, stating, "She will be set free when judged by God. It's important that she die in incarceration." Pam Turner, a cousin of Sharon Tate, also opposed Atkins' release, stating, "If she were capable of comprehending what our family's been through, she would be ashamed to come before this parole board and ask such a request." Anthony DiMaria, the nephew of murder victim Thomas Jay Sebring, also opposed Atkins' release, stating, "You will hear various opinions with respect to this today, but you will hear nothing from the nine people who lie in their graves and suffered horrendous deaths at the hands of Susan Atkins."

Gloria Goodwin Killian, director of ACWIP (Action Committee for Women in Prison) and a Pasadena legal researcher and prisoner advocate, spoke in support for Atkins' compassionate release, arguing, "Susan has been punished all that she can be. Short of going out to the hospital and physically torturing her, there is nothing left anyone can do to her. The people who are suffering are the people you see in this room today." In July 2008, Atkins' husband, James W. Whitehouse, told the board, "They tell me we're lucky if we have three months. It's not going to be fun. It's not going to be pretty."

The 11 members of the California Board of Parole Hearings ultimately denied Atkins' request in a unanimous decision after final deliberations. The decision — posted on its Web site — meant the Atkins' request would not be forwarded to the Los Angeles Superior Court that sentenced her, which would have had the final say as to whether or not she would be released. On September 24, 2008, Atkins was transferred back to the Central California Women's Facility in Chowchilla, California to the facility's skilled nursing center.

Prior to her 2009 parole hearing, a website maintained by Atkins' husband claimed that she was paralyzed over 85 percent of her body and unable to sit up or be transferred to a wheelchair.

For the eighteenth and final time, Atkins was denied parole on September 2, 2009. On September 3, the parole board denied her release. She would have been able to try again in 2012, but died on Thursday September 24, 2009, at the Central California Women's facility in Chowchilla. A prison spokesman announced to reporters that her cause of death was listed as natural causes because her family did not request an autopsy. Her husband, James Whitehouse, subsequently released the following statement: "Susan passed away peacefully surrounded by friends and loved ones and the incredible staff at the Skilled Nursing Facility at the Central California Women's Facility ... Her last whispered word was 'Amen.' "

On September 3, the parole board denied her release. She would have been able to try again in 2012, but died on Thursday September 24, 2009.

Patricia "Katie" Krenwinkel

Patricia "Katie" Krenwinkel Then

Patricia "Katie" Krenwinkel Now

Krenwinkel, still incarcerated, is now at the California Institution for Women in Chino, California. In an interview conducted by Diane Sawyer in 1994, Krenwinkel stated: "I wake up every day knowing that I'm a destroyer of the most precious thing, which is life; and I do that because that's what I deserve, is to wake up every morning and know that." During that same interview, Patricia expressed the most remorse for what she did to Folger, telling Diane Sawyer, "That was just a young woman that I killed, who had parents. She was supposed to live a life and her parents were never supposed to see her dead."

During a 2004 parole hearing, when asked who she would place at the top of the list of people she has harmed, Patricia Krenwinkel responded, "Myself." She was denied parole following that hearing because, according to the panel, Krenwinkel still posed an "unacceptable risk to public safety". In total, Krenwinkel has been denied parole thirteen times; her last hearing was in January 2011. The two-member parole board said after the hearing in Los Angeles that the 63-year-old Krenwinkel would not be eligible for parole again for seven years. The panel said they were swayed by the memory of the crimes, along with 80 letters which came from all over the world urging Patricia Krenwinkel's continued incarceration.

Krenwinkel, is the longest-serving female prisoner in the California prison system — a distinction she gained when fellow Charles Manson follower Susan Atkins died in 2009.

Linda Kasabian

Linda Kasabian Then

Linda Kasabian Now

Linda Kasabian was granted immunity for giving evidence against Manson and other family members. Following the trial she left California.

The heavy news media coverage of the Manson trial had made Linda Kasabian a well-known, if somewhat controversial, figure by the time the sentences had been handed down, with opinions about her ranging from sympathetic to hostile. Kasabian shortly returned to New Hampshire with her husband and her children, seeking to escape the glare of the media, and to raise her children quietly. She lived on a hippie commune for a time and worked as a cook later.

Kasabian was called back to Los Angeles County several times after the first trial: she was a witness against Tex Watson in his separate trial in 1971, and also against Leslie Van Houten in her two retrials in 1977. Linda Kasabian later divorced her husband Robert Kasabian, and eventually she remarried.

Kasabian was detained for numerous traffic violations, until an automobile accident left her partially disabled. During an Easter celebration in New Hampshire in 1978, she and some friends interfered with firemen who were attempting to extinguish a bonfire. Though she had severed all of her ties with the Manson "family", the Secret Service kept her under surveillance for a time after her former Manson associate Lynette "Squeaky" Fromme attempted to assassinate President Gerald Ford. Kasabian was the target of scorn from the few remaining Manson "family" members.

Over the years, Kasabian has avoided and refused most news media attention. She appeared only once from 1969 to 2008, for an interview with the syndicated American television program *A Current Affair* in 1988.

Most recently, Cineflix, a production company in the United Kingdom and Canada, produced a docu-drama called *Manson*, in which Kasabian appears, telling her story in complete detail for the first time. This program was telecast in the UK on August 10, 2009, and also in the United States on Sept. 7, 2009 and again on July 20, 2013, on the History Channel. In this taped interview, Kasabian recounts her four weeks spent with the Manson "family". Her image is slightly obscured to protect her identity.

In a September 2, 2009 live interview on CNN's *Larry King Live*, Kasabian recounted her memories of the murders at Sharon Tate's home. To help her maintain her now-quiet life, Kasabian wore a disguise provided by the program during her interview. She told King during the interview that after the trial she had been in need of, but had never obtained, "psychological counseling", and that during the previous 12 years, she had been "on a path of healing and rehabilitation." When asked about the degree of remorse she felt for her participation in the crimes, Kasabian said that she felt as though she took on all the guilt that "no one else who was involved in the crimes felt guilt for", apparently referring to the fact that, even during her own court testimony, the co-defendants in the case showed extreme nonchalance when faced with such gruesome murders.

Sandra Good

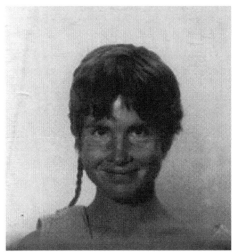

Sandra Good Then

Sandra Good Now

On December 22, 1975, Good and another Manson devotee, Susan Murphy, were indicted for "conspiracy to send threatening letters through the mail" by a Federal Grand Jury in Sacramento, in connection with death threats against more than 170 corporate executives who Good believed (see ATWA) were polluting the earth.

Found guilty on March 16, 1976, Good was sentenced on April 13, to 15 years in prison.

Good was paroled in early December 1985, after having served nearly 10 years. Unlike many of the Family members, Good still professed total allegiance to Manson.

A stipulation of her parole was that she could not return to California. She moved to Vermont, where she lived quietly under the name Sandra Collins until 1989, when her environmental activism made the news and her identity was made public.

After her time on parole ended, Good moved to Hanford, California, near Corcoran State Prison, to be closer to Manson, although she was not allowed to visit him. On January 26, 1996, she and George Stimson began a pro-Manson website, on which they claimed to have the true source of Manson thought. She also supported Manson's environmental movement, ATWA (Air Trees Water Animals). The website went offline in 2001, but in 2011 Good's website was relaunched.

Sandra Good has since left Hanford, and she and Stimson have made no public statements in support of Manson.

Steve "Clem" Grogan

Steve "Clem" Grogan Then

Steve "Clem" Grogan Now

Grogan later helped Manson, Watson and Bruce Davis to

kill Spahn ranch hand Donald "Shorty" Shea. The jury returned verdicts of life imprisonment for Manson and Davis, but death for Grogan. However, on December 23, 1971, Judge James Kolts stated that "Grogan was too stupid and too hopped on drugs to decide anything on his own" and that it was really Manson "who decided who lived or died" and reduced Grogan's sentence to life imprisonment. Grogan later assisted the authorities and drew a map to where Shea's body was buried. In prison he was head of the prison's program to deter juveniles from a life of crime and kept away from fellow inmate Manson. Grogan also played guitar and sang in the Freedom Orchestra Band with fellow Manson family co-conspirator Bobby Beausoleil when they both served time at the Deuel Vocational Institute in Tracy, California. Beausoleil later revealed that he convinced Grogan to begin playing again and even made him a guitar. He was released from prison in 1985 and remains the only Manson family member who has been convicted of murder and released from prison.

Bruce Davis

Bruce Davis Then

Bruce Davis Now

Bruce Davis is serving a life sentence in the California Men's Colony, San Luis Obispo, for the murders of Gary Hinman and Donald Shea. He attended his twenty seventh parole hearing in March of 2013. Parole was again refused.

Mr. Davis would have been only the second Manson-related murder convict to be granted parole since the killings began in 1969.

In March 2013, Gov. Jerry Brown reversed a parole board and denied release of Bruce Davis who has served more than 40 years in prison.

The board had recently approved the release of 70-year-old Bruce Davis but left the final decision to the governor.

Brown gave his decision to The Associated Press at the downtown Los Angeles County courthouse after a meeting with District Attorney Jackie Lacey.

"I find the evidence ... shows why he currently poses a danger to society if released from prison. Therefore, I reverse the decision to parole Mr. Davis," the written decision said.

Davis was not involved in the notorious Sharon Tate-LaBianca killings but was convicted with Manson and others in the murders of Gary Hinman and Donald Shea.

Steve Grogan, another participant in those murders, was released many years ago after he agreed to lead police to where the bodies were buried on a remote movie ranch in the San Fernando Valley.

Davis was 30 when he was sentenced to life in prison in 1972 in the case that was a postscript to Manson's notorious reign as leader of the murderous communal cult known as the Manson family.

Davis long maintained that he was a bystander in the killings of the two men, but in recent years, he has acknowledged his shared responsibility

Davis became a born-again Christian in prison and ministered to other inmates, married a woman he met through the prison ministry, and has a grown daughter. The couple recently divorced. Davis also earned a master's degree and a doctorate in philosophy of religion.

Bobby Beausoleil

Bobby Beausoleil Then

Bobby Beausoleil Now

Convicted in 1969 for his part in the murder of Gary Hinman, he remains in prison despite numerous appeals and bail applications. He married in 1982 and is currently serving out his time in Oregon after being transferred there in 1993 at his own request.

It seems, Bobby Beausoleil was something of an entrepreneur back in 1984. He was apparently running a business out of his prison cell called "B & B Enterprises." The company consisted of himself, of course, and his wife, according to prison officials. An actual lieutenant from the prison security team at CMC wrote Beausoleil up, and filled out a report, which is summarized here:

"Approximately mid-December of 1984 Inmate Beausoleil received in the institution mail a large manila envelope containing Xerox copies of the following. Number one, letters of correspondence with people from various states. These letters pertained to purchase orders of child pornography, ages between four and 12 years old. The types of orders were photographs, movies, tape cassettes and magazines. They were all specific as to what they preferred, age, sex and nationality. Two, photocopies of order forms with names and addresses of purchasers with their money order or check made out to B&B Enterprise. A few money orders were made out to R. Beausoleil in care of B&B Enterprises. Three, one letter pertained to a person offering his services to B&B Enterprise by making movies or magazines for him, meaning Beausoleil. In this letter the man stated that he and an accomplice kidnapped children between the ages of four and eight years old. They moved from one state to another every three months to stay ahead of the law. Some states he mentioned were Florida,

Washington DC, Colorado, and the last state in which they had just left was Arizona. He mentioned after their stay in California they were heading to Washington. Four, photocopies of bank records showing deposits to B&B Enterprise and R. Beausoleil. All of this information came with a return address of B&B Enterprise, P.O. Box 1033 in Grover City." Which I believe is where Mr. Beausoleil's wife was living at the time. "In the second week of February, Inmate Beausoleil received another manila envelope from B&B Enterprise in Grover City. This envelope contained purchase orders for magazines containing -- which contained nothing but child spanking and beatings. Each one asked for a certain age, sex and nationality. The order forms were addressed to Sassy Bottoms, B&B Enterprises, P.O. Box 1033, Grover City, California 93433."

He has spent his 30-plus years in prison focused on electronic music and video production. He has also cultivated a number of sponsors, which has resulted in the creation of a video production and audio recording studio in the prison. He is now the director of the Los Hermanos video project and has made 9 videos for "at risk" children. He has also made videos that help prisoners develop cognitive skills that will hopefully reduce recidivism.

10050 Cielo Drive

10050 Cielo Drive in 1969

10050 Cielo Drive (now 10066 **Cielo Drive**), as it looks today

The Crime Scene

According to an August 1999 *Reuters* news service report the house at 10050 Cielo Drive, rented by Roman Polanski and Sharon Tate at the time of the murders, was demolished in 1994.   An Italian- style mansion has been erected in its place and the street address has been changed. The new mansion was originally priced at $12.5 million in an attempt to cash in on the locations notoriety but no sale was made.   Recently, the price was reduced to $7.7 million but the house still remains vacant.

3301 Waverly Drive

3301 Waverly Drive Then

3301 Waverly Drive now

The address was changed to 3311 Waverly drive and a second driveway and a gate has since been added to the property.

Spahn Ranch

Spahn Ranch in 1969

Spahn Ranch as it looks today

The original headquarters of the Manson family is also on the market. The 43-acre property at Chatsworth, minus the ranch house, which burnt down some time ago, is selling for $2.7 million.

Bibliography

Breault, Marc, with Martin King. *Inside the Cult.* New York: Signet. 1993.

FBI, "Report to the Deputy Attorney General on the Events at Waco, Texas," www.usdojgov.com

Linedecker, Clifford. *Massacre at Waco, Texas.* New York: St. Martin's Press, 1993.

Moran, Sarah. *The Secret World of Cults.* Surrey, England: CLB International, 1999.

Twentieth Century with Mike Wallace: Cults, The History Channel, 1996.

Wessinger, Catherine. *How the Millennium Comes Violently.* New York: Seven Bridges Press, 2000.

Whitcomb, Christopher. *Cold Zero: Inside the FBI Hostage Rescue Team.* New York: Little, brown, & Co., 2001.

Freedberg, Sydney P. *Brother Love: Murder, Money, and a Messiah*, New York: Pantheon Books. 1994.

Clary, Mike. "Sect Leader Stands Trial in Slayings," *Los Angeles Times*, 1992

Clary, Mike. "Charismatic Sect Leader Tied to 'Reign of Terror,'" *Los Angeles Times.* January 26, 1991

DallasMorning News. "From Pro Athlete to Religious Fanatic and Murder Suspect," December 4, 1986.

Longa, Lyda. "Sect's Service Center Saves More Than Souls," *Fort Lauderdale Sun-Sentinel*, December 3, 1989.

Murphy, Brian. "Mysterious 'Son of God' Courts the Lords of Business," *Associated Press*. July 29, 1990.

Williams, Mike. "Cult Leader Faces Trial on 14 Murder Counts," *The Atlanta Journal and The Atlanta Constitution*. January 2, 1992.

Williams, Mike. "Cult Leader Charmed Miami Until Murder Charges. Yahweh sect linked to extortion, 14 killings," *The Atlanta Journal and The Atlanta Constitution*. November 11, 1990.

Transcript, Eleventh Circuit Court of Appeals, UNITED STATES of America v. Robert Louis BEASLEY, Jr. aka "Dan Israel," et al. Jan. 5, 1996.

"Cults," *Twentieth Century with Mike Wallace*. The History Channel, 1996.

Henry, William. *The Keepers of Heaven's Gate: The Millennial Madness*. Anchorage, AK: Earthpulse Press, 1997.

Holliman, John. "Applewhite: From Young Overachiever to Cult Leader," CNN.com./specials/1998/.

Krueger, Anne, and Susan Gembrowski, "Strange odyssey of Heaven's Gate," *San Diego Union-Tribune*. April 13, 1997.

Moran, Sarah. *The Secret World of Cults*. Surrey, England: CLB International, 1999.

"The Next Level," *Newsweek*, April 7, 1997.

Thornton, Kelly, and Susan Gembrowski, "Cult claims two new victims," *San Diego Union-Tribune*, May 7, 1997.

Wessinger, Catherine. *How the Millennium Comes Violently*. New York: Seven Bridges Press, 2000.

"A Beautiful Dream Turned Into a Deadly Nightmare" by Jynona Norwood

"The Jonestown Massacre" Author unknown

"Jonestown Suicides Shocked World" *By The Associated Press* Thursday, March 27, 1997; 1:00 p.m. EST

"Making Sense of the Nonsensical: An Analysis of Jonestown" By Neal Osherow

"Jonestown massacre + 20: Questions linger" November 18, 1998 Web posted at: 12:56 p.m. EST (1756 GMT) Author unknown

"Newly Released Documents Shed Light on Unsolved Murders" by Thomas G. Whittle and Jan Thorpe Official Documentation

"The Assassination Of Representative Leo J. Ryan and The Jonestown, Guyana Tragedy" Report of a Staff Investigative Group to The Committee on

Foreign Affairs U.S. House of Representatives
May 15, 1979

Affidavit of Deborah Layton Blakey re the Threat and
Possibility of Mass Suicide
by Members of the People's Temple.

Testimony of Clare Bouquet Before The International
Operations Subcommittee,
Committee On Foreign Affairs
February 20, 1980

Look for these and other great books
By David Pietras

From "Mommy to Monster"

The "Daddy Dearest" Club

The Manson Family "Then and Now"

When Love Kills

The Making of a Nightmare

THE INFAMOUS "FLORIDA 5"

Death, Murder, and Vampires Real Vampire Stories

The Life and Death of Richard Ramirez, The Night Stalker
(History's Killers Unmasked Series)

Profiling The Killer of a Childhood Beauty Queen

No Justice For Caylee Anthony

A Texas Style Witch Hunt "Justice Denied" The Darlie
Lynn Routier Story by

The Book of Revelations Explained The End Times

Murder of a Childhood

John Gotti: A True Mafia Don (History's Killers Unmasked
Series)

MURDERED FOR HIS MILLIONS The Abraham
Shakespeare Case

The Son of Sam "Then and Now" The David Berkowitz
Story

A LOOK INSIDE THE FIVE MAFIA FAMILIES OF
NEW YORK CITY

Unmasking The Real Hannibal Lecter

Top 10 Most Haunted Places in America

40 minutes in Abbottabad The Raid on Osama bin Laden

In The Footsteps of a Hero The Military Journey of General
David H. Petraeus

BATTLEFIELD BENGHAZI

CASE CLOSED The State of Florida vs. George
Zimmerman THE TRUTH REVEALED

CROSSING THE THIN BLUE LINE

THE GHOST FROM MY CHILDHOOD A TRUE
GHOST STORY ABOUT THE GELSTON CASTLE AND
THE GHOST OF "AUNT" HARRIET DOUGLAS...

Haunted United Kingdom

In Search of Jack the Ripper (History's Killers Unmasked
Series)

The Last Ride of Bonnie and Clyde

The Meaning of a Tragedy Canada's Serial Killers Revealed

MOMSTER

Murder In The Kingdom

The Shroud of Turin and the Mystery Surrounding Its Authenticity

The Unexplained World That We Live In

The Good, The Bad and The Gunslingers

MOMSTERS Mothers Who Kill Their Children

KIDNAPPED A Parent's Worst Nightmare

Saving Angels

The Ghosts of Shawshank

The Tragic Little Pageant Princess

FOREVER MANSON

Made In New York City

Innocent on Death Row

Happy Father's Day

Dr Death M.D.

From "Fugitive" to Freedom

Tears of our Fathers

Most Haunted Crime Scenes in the World

America's Monsters

No Mommy Don't

Ghosts of The United Kingdom

The Last Don of New York City

Inside The NYC Mafia

Unanswered Evidence

Deadly Faith

8946470R00135

Printed in Great Britain
by Amazon.co.uk, Ltd.,
Marston Gate.